BREAKOUT

Surviving Abuse and Alcoholism. This is My Story.

Sukree Boodram

Confidential
No copying or sharing without written consent from author

Copyright © 2010 Sukree Boodram
All rights reserved.

ISBN: 0615364578
ISBN-13: 9780615364575
Library of Congress Control Number: 2010932177

*You may never know what results come of your action,
but if you do nothing there will be no result.*

                                                                —Gandhi

www.sukreeboodram.com

For my dad, may he rest in peace,

and

my two beautiful children, Randy and Sam

Contents

Author's Note · · · · · · · · · · · · · · · · · xi
Introduction · · · · · · · · · · · · · · · · · · 1
Life's First Memories · · · · · · · · · · · · · 5
Growing Up Fast · · · · · · · · · · · · · · · · 9
Death of a Legend · · · · · · · · · · · · · · 13
Dreams of All Young Girls · · · · · · · · · 17
The One · 19
Life in the Big City · · · · · · · · · · · · · · 25
Living Life on Life's Terms · · · · · · · · · 29
Life's New Experiences · · · · · · · · · · · 33
Dog Days of Heaven · · · · · · · · · · · · · 35
Good Riddance · · · · · · · · · · · · · · · · 39
Start of a Union · · · · · · · · · · · · · · · · 41
Leaping into Life · · · · · · · · · · · · · · · 43
The Wedding · · · · · · · · · · · · · · · · · · 47
The Lost Years · · · · · · · · · · · · · · · · 51
Hello Florida · · · · · · · · · · · · · · · · · · 55
Nothing Beats Higher Education · · · · 61
The Grand Entrance · · · · · · · · · · · · · 65
Thoughts of a Breakup · · · · · · · · · · · 69
My Miracle Child · · · · · · · · · · · · · · · 75
A New Beginning · · · · · · · · · · · · · · · 79
Early Years in Howey in the Hills · · · 83
The Longest Ending · · · · · · · · · · · · · 87
An Animal's Instinct · · · · · · · · · · · · · 91
A New Career · · · · · · · · · · · · · · · · · 95

Personality Changes	99
Taking Charge of My Life	103
An Unforgettable Start to 2007	107
Post Baker Act	113
Test of Faith	117
My Darkest Days	121
S.T.O.P.	127
Peace vs. Chaos: A Day in Court	131
Facing the Truth: Alcoholism	135
Rehab	143
Face-off at Rehab	147
Back to Familiar Grounds	151
A Mother's Love	155
Trying to Fake It	159
A Test of Change	163
The Final Breakup	167
Negotiating the Divorce	171
Doomsday of Divorce	177
Me and my Higher Power	181
Divorce and Family	185
The Final Last Chance	189
The First Last Vacation	193
The Last Failed Control	197
The Last Confrontation	203
The Last Farewell	207
Reflections	211
Epilogue	217

Acknowledgments

*In this life we cannot do great things. We can
only do small things with great love.*
—Mother Teresa

Thank you, thank you, thank you to the people who read, reread, and read some more drafts of this book:

Lakhram Boodram, devoted first editor and confidant

Ninawattie Budhram, my soundboard

Ninasattie Singh, sister and loyal supporter

Udesh Laikhram, exceptionally patient nephew

Dindeah Persaud, sister thinking outside the box

Drupati Boodram, lending me my first editor, her husband

Padmini Boodram, for her contributions to grammar and layout

Natasha Swampillai, first manuscript reviewer

Jeremy Swampillai, first manuscript reviewer

Paul Trepte, first manuscript reviewer

Special thanks to:

my mom for making it possible for me to educate myself at a time when it was financially difficult for our family.

Not forgetting the dedication of:

Max Schilling, 1st Web designer

Jessie Matanky, 2nd Web designer

Stephanie Pachaeo, photographer

Joseph Seagle, PA

CreateSpace, partners in getting my book published

Finally, to all my loyal friends for their support; you know who you are.

Author's Note

As I was finishing this manuscript, I took some time off from work during the last two weeks of 2009. My children were in Canada on vacation, and I was home alone. I wanted to take the time to think about my decision to publish this book. A question of concern popped into my mind: how would this impact my children, and how would it impact their dad?

I pondered that question for days. At times, I came close to not going through with the project. Then I remembered a quote I had for years on my refrigerator: *Stand up for your principles, even if you are left standing alone.* I am not sure who said it or where it came from, but it encouraged me to revisit my apprehension about publishing my story.

Days later, I made the final decision to proceed with publishing because I want others in similar circumstances to know there are others out there like them. I want to share where I obtained my help and to educate them on how I extricated myself from an unhealthy situation and started living a healthier life. I knew the cost would be a factor, but I thought if my book helped to inspire one person, especially in my cultural community, the cost would be justified. So, I proceeded with publishing at the end of 2009.

I realize there are risks in every decision I make, and there could be risks associated with telling my story. However, not telling my story would be not using my life experiences in a positive way to inspire others who may be in a similar position. I want to share my struggles, my heartaches, and my ultimate survival of an abusive relationship with an alcoholic husband.

I am not an expert on the subject matter of abuse or alcoholism. I am not proclaiming to have formally educated myself on how an abuser or alcoholic thinks. I know only from experience. I am an accountant by career, a mom by choice, and I aspire to be a kind and caring person in our society. This is my story, and it represents my perceptions and opinions based on how I was treated in my marriage. I have based it on facts and incidents I experienced as I remembered and interpreted them at the time. This is about my feelings, thoughts, and actions. It does not represent or claim to represent how others may have felt, their state of mind, or their intent. It is my perception only.

This book is not intended to be a substitute for therapy or professional advice. All attempts have been made to verify information on dates, though some may not be correct. Any perceived slight of specific people or organizations is unintentional. Any self-help contents are solely my opinion and should not be considered as a form of therapy, advice, direction, and/or diagnosis or treatment of any kind: medical, spiritual, mental, or other. If expert advice or counseling is needed, services of a competent professional should be sought. I assume no responsibility or liability and specifically disclaim any warranty, express or implied, for any self-help or otherwise. A purchaser or reader of this book assumes responsibility for the use of any materials and information contained herein.

With that said, we can now move on. Warm wishes and welcome to my book.

—Sukree

Introduction

How many people do you know from Black Bush Polder, Guyana, South America, with conservative, traditional Hindu values? If you were born in that corner of the world, I would guess a whole lot. OK then, how many are willing to tell you their life stories, possibly enduring the shame, humiliation, and criticism that accompany the most sacred things we are taught to preserve, our private lives? I am sure not many. You are about to meet me, Sukree Boodram. I was born at Lot 50 Joanna North, Black Bush Polder, Guyana, South America.

So where is Guyana? It is located in the West Indies in the upper northeastern part of South America, bordering the Atlantic Ocean. Even though I am of East Indian descent, I am a West Indian by birth.

A brief history of my country: first occupied by Spain in 1499, Guyana came under Dutch control by the mid-1700s. The British gained possession of Guyana in 1814, which brought a large influx of East Indians. The country is now called The Cooperative Republic of Guyana, after gaining its independence from the British.

Guyana is one of the few English-speaking countries in South America. It is set like a gem in the crown of the continent, nestled alongside and defying the rages of the Atlantic Ocean. The country has numerous waterways and it is commonly referred to as "The Land of Many Waters."

My beloved village is beautiful. It is comprised of hundreds of acres of fields traversed by numerous canals and waterways. Farming areas are dotted with small, widely spaced homes, the abodes of working families. It is as rural as it gets. You go to bed when the sun goes down and rise with it. The sound of nature encompasses it all.

I attended Multi Lateral High School in the city of New Amsterdam, and later graduated from Winifred Gaskin Memorial High. I graduated at the top of my class, and yes, I would consider myself something of a nerd back then—not now, of course. My friends would say otherwise, but what do they know?

For as long as I can remember, I've loved reading. As a child growing up, I felt the need to read and read and read some more. I used to read any books, magazines, or newspapers I could find. However, my choice of reading materials was limited since exciting, interesting, and current materials were almost nonexistent back then.

My earliest recollection of the joys of reading is of my dad reading newspapers that were many weeks or even months old. You see, news of current events was a luxury. Local gossips were generally the main source of current news. I used to sit and watch my dad read really "big" words. I was impressed by his intelligence. From my love of reading came the art of writing. Hence, was born this wonderful story of life's struggles, life's surprises, and life's accomplishments.

When I was still young, my dad told me that I was special and different. He told me that someday I would marry a "good man" and be happy. He told me I was the prettiest girl he had ever seen, and that one day I would travel the world and be rich in all things. I believed every word of it.

Unknown to me at the time, he was simply trying to make me want to be around him with old-fashioned bribery. You see, my dad was disabled most of my life, and I was the last of many siblings, so I ended up getting the luxury of staying home with him in case he needed anything. I loved it. I had no other friends; my dad was my one and only best friend. He was the first one I saw when I got up and the last one I saw when I went to bed. He was my life. He made my life. He made me what I am today.

I am the last of thirteen siblings from three marriages. My dad's first marriage produced five children. They are much older than I am, and by the time I came along, they were married with a few kids or they had moved away. My mom's first marriage produced three children. Likewise, by the time I was born, they were also married or they had moved away. My mom and dad went on to have five children, of which I am the last and probably the most pampered. Fortunately, I grew up with four other siblings and both my parents in my home. My brothers were born first. The eldest is Lakhram, followed by Shammie. Then three of us sisters came along: Devika followed by Puchie then finally, several years later, the accidental child. That would be me. I guess when I came along my parents took one look at me and agreed I was the perfect child—no need to have another. Apparently, birth control was either not an option back then or rarely utilized.

Introduction

Life for me was not easy. I plan to take you through the struggles of being born into a family of overwhelming courage, a society of virtually no middle class, and the personal struggles to overcome all odds. I believe I was born with the gift of being the best at what I endeavored to do. I wanted to be the best in school and do the right thing by everyone, even if I suffered. My dad taught me this. I hope you will be challenged to become the best of what you aspire to be. My cherished hope is that we all live with grace, humility, and kindness amid the almost constant turbulence of the world. I also hope you have or will like and fall in love with the person you see in the mirror each day. I hope I am able to touch the lives of my readers and encourage everyone, when faced with adversities, to stop, think clearly, and then act appropriately, specifically in that order, without hurting others.

My life's first memories, tragically, were of my dad's struggle to stay alive. I heard a woman saying, *"...get the towel...he is bleeding...lay him flat on the ground...hope the car comes soon...he might die."*

At age four, I stood there looking on as my mother and our neighbors waited for a car to come by to take my dad to the hospital. It was 1970. We waited by the roadside with one car passing every hour or so in this very remote and isolated community. I remember only the blood and fragments of conversations. This was the first memory of my life, and the images will never leave. What a grand start to my adventurous journey from childhood to adulthood.

I later learned my dad had suffered three prior heart attacks. This was the fourth one. From my recollection and conversations with my mom and older siblings, the last attack resulted in his disability. I remembered him having continuous breathing issues and extreme exhaustion from simple steps he would attempt to take.

My dad became mostly bedridden from then on. The next nine years until his death were marked with struggles to survive, the will to live, and the few moments of joy we found with him. His mental state and the ability to teach us did not cease until the last year of his life. Thinking back now, perhaps his illness was God's way of keeping my father home in order to allow us an opportunity to learn from him. Those nine years taught me about simplicity, love, and controversies. Those years taught me about pain, how speedily one person can carelessly hurt another without even knowing it.

Please open your minds and your hearts to a wonderful, true story. As the story unfolds, you may cry and perhaps laugh. Most importantly, it might make you think about your own life and stimulate you to plan for the years ahead. I will share with you choices and heartbreaks I would have never dreamed of as a child. It might prompt you to show humility and thankfulness for the things you have. At times, like me, under the influence of intense bliss, you might feel like dancing without the sound of music. Let's begin my journey together.

Life's First Memories

*I thank my mother and father each day
for what they taught me.*

We lived in a two-story Caribbean stilt-style home situated on 2.5 acres surrounded by an abundance of fruit trees and wildlife. There were three bedrooms and living areas on the upper level with the kitchen and dining area on the lower level. We had a very large area around our home built with covered barns and sheds for the safekeeping of our animals. Growing up it was a joy to be surrounded by our animals from house pets to cattle, which my parents raised commercially. Our household was a constant hustle and bustle from feeding the animals to learning how to tend to the newborns. An opportunity I still treasure.

As a child, I remember sitting on the upper balcony with my four siblings and listening to the tales my father used to tell of his childhood years and the things he encountered. He was keen in his choice of words and descriptive enough to scare the pants off a five-year-old. Growing up, I used to wonder about his stories. He probably made some up; nevertheless, I was entertained and extremely scared at times.

After several heart attacks, at age fifty-nine my father became disabled. He sat down a lot and could not walk any distance without becoming exhausted. He did minor tasks around the home, such as fishing in the nearby waterways in order kill time. Being the youngest, I was assigned the duty as Dad's sitter. I thought at the time I was special and had been awarded the honor of spending all my time with Dad. Later I learned no one else may have wanted the job.

We had to perform several chores to help Dad, such as bringing him food and water, massaging his feet and back, and helping him get up and down the stairs. We had to do everything for him, and most children my age wanted to be out getting into trouble with their friends. Not me, I wanted to be home with Dad. I loved my dad more that anything. He kept me entertained, and most of all, he showed me how to love unconditionally.

My sense of determination and adaptation started early. This was my life, not a dream, not figments of my imagination, simply life. My life was as simple as it gets. Fortunately, I had not yet polluted my mind; it was pure and innocent.

In the evenings, one of my older sisters would start dinner, or if my mom were home, she would tend to the task. But my mom was rarely home; she was out "bringing home the bacon." The few moments we had with her were in the form of her telling us what to do, how to do it, and when to do it. This was her role. It was fair to say she was the "man of the house." The loving and cuddling was left up to Dad, as he was always home.

This is not how a typical family in my culture functions. The father is expected to be the sole provider and the mother, the loyal and obedient homemaker. My mom graciously took on the role of provider after my dad became disabled. Looking back now, I realize my mom was one of few women I knew of at the time who played this role in our culture. She definitely earns my respect for stepping up to the plate and taking care of her family.

Life was good back then. We had family, food, clothing, and a place to live. Little did I know that my mother had to contend with other things. Things like ensuring that we girls went to school and didn't get into trouble or go off with boys and get pregnant! That was a task all its own. God forbade girls to have intercourse before marriage. If we did, we were sure not to find a man to marry us. Mom made this clear.

My dad was an entertainer and an educator. He was intelligent beyond words. That said, he never went to college. At that time, there were no colleges in Guyana. However, he taught us the meaning of life through his storytelling. Dad would tell us stories of other families going through "suffering" because their children were "bad." He taught us how to think, plan, and execute decisions through card games. He taught us how to make decisions based on our knowledge. He trained us to think ahead, know whom we were playing against and their motives, and then play to win. He taught us to make accurate assessments of the opponent's hand and be time conscious, proactive, and patient; to know when to walk away from a game and to do it with grace and dignity, never with resentment. Little did I know then, these were life lessons Dad was teaching us. He taught me almost everything I needed to know to lead a successful life. It was all he could give me. It was all I needed.

Dad's life was definitely unbearable. He could not walk or lie down. It was very difficult for him to breathe. We had to help him to bed and around the house. We did everything for our dad and never complained much. I never knew all this time I was learning how to love, how to give, and how to care without looking for anything in return. My father taught me to give without expecting rewards and to strive for happiness; he showed me what unconditional love looks like.

My mother and father are the first two teachers from whom I was privileged to learn. I love them both, and they have taught me much of what to do and not do.

Growing Up Fast

Time waits for no one.

Nothing changed for years, but the years went by. My oldest brother, Lakhram, completed high school. He later went on to be a teacher. My next-oldest brother, Shammie, finished school and continued the family business of farming. My oldest sister, Devika, finished school and later also started teaching. My immediate oldest sister and to date my best friend, Puchie, went to high school with me. We graduated one after the other.

In the fall of 1979, my dad was getting progressively worse. His health was deteriorating at a rapid rate. I was thirteen years old at the time. My mother was spending a large amount of time taking him to the hospitals in the area in hopes of finding a doctor who would operate on his heart. It was clear the end was near. There was little hope that an operation would be a success.

In October 1979, Dad came home from a long hospital stay. The doctors had told my mom to bring him home for the remaining days of his life. He was about to die. My brothers went to get my dad from the taxi that had brought him home from the hospital. I was very anxious; I could not wait to see my dad. He had been at the hospital almost a month, and I rarely saw him. Finally, my father, my friend, my buddy was coming back.

When he arrived, he looked frail and ill, but I didn't care, I wanted him back home to sit and tell me stories again. At thirteen, only the little things matter. My dad was back, and I said to myself that as soon as he saw me, he would take one look at me and realize how much he missed me. Everything would be great!

My brothers pulled into the front of the house, and I ran to see my dad. My mom and brothers were busy trying to take him bed. We all gathered around watching him. He looked at us and said,

"Are these all my children?"

What? He did not know me? How was it possible? This was not real. I felt alone. I wanted to scream.

"Yes, these are your children," my mom said.

I finally realized my dad was really, really sick. He had lost his memory. Imagine this: he had been ill and bedridden for years prior to that day, but I never saw his illness. I saw only what I wanted to see, a man of endurance, love, and a lot to give me. The pure joy and fun listening to all the stories of his childhood was now gone. I clearly remember telling myself, *Life is not what it seems to be.*

I stayed quiet for a long time after that day. I stayed close to Dad and started to plan my future at thirteen. I knew I was alone, and my dad was no longer around to teach me. I had to take care of myself. I had to take what I learned from him and define the rest of my life. I had to move forward. There would be no looking back. The past was history I could not change. At thirteen, this is what I thought. The years of teachings my dad provided me, I realized, were to prepare me for the rest of my life. He knew he would die long before I grew up to take care of myself.

As the months went by, I kept mostly to myself and, when I could, close to my dad sitting or reading next to him. Toward the end of December, my dad was getting worse. He was not eating or sleeping, and we could not take care of him any longer. The week between Christmas and New Year's he returned to the New Amsterdam Public Hospital; the city was some distance from home. My mom had found a doctor who would operate on his heart. This was the last attempt to prolong his life.

Right after the New Year, my mother came home and said she was not sure the surgery would help Dad or even if he would live until the surgery. He was not cooperating and did not want the surgery. He did not want to put us through the pain and expense. He told my mother he was ready to die.

School had started, and Puchie and I were excited to be back. For us, school was happiness. We were away from home and away from heartaches. Friends, I learned, can be a good source of distraction from the things that cause us pain, a lesson that would benefit me later in my life, and a lifeline I use quite often today.

On January 8, 1980, two weeks after my mom took my dad to the hospital, he died. He was sixty-seven years old. A nurse later told my mom on the night of his departure that he constantly called out the names of his children. He had remembered us. We were called from school and went home. I had no tears, no pain, and no sorrow. I was glad my dad had died. Strange, isn't it? Even though I loved my Dad and would miss him, I was happy he was no longer suffering and that I would no longer have to see him suffer.

Everyone was busy during the funeral, so no one noticed I did not cry. I went along with whatever was going on. I kept wake with everyone, I ate with everyone, and I listened to the pundits (a Hindu holy person) with everyone. But I was lost. Everything I did and every decision I made, my dad had had input. We would decide together what we would eat, when we would eat, and what we would do next. I felt lost, as my guidance was lost. Ironically, as I was writing my book, my brothers and sisters confessed that they did not cry either.

The few days of wake and funeral went by quickly. I told myself I would never depend on anyone again because I would never feel the pain again when a person I loved decided to leave, either by death or otherwise. Little did I know at that young age that emotions are meant to be felt. They are the elements that make us who we are and define humility in us.

Sometimes we set our expectations too high or expect something without first understanding a situation. I have learned not to expect too much, but to accept life on life's terms.

Death of a Legend

The blessings of my good father flow even after death.

In what seemed like an instant, our household went from seven to three. On January 12, 1980, my dad was laid to rest. On February 10, 1980, Lakhram got married to beautiful Shirley and moved out. In September 1980, Devika went off to a university in England. She later became a registered nurse. In January 1981, Shammie went to Texas Southern University. This left Puchie, Mom, and me alone in a huge home.

This was a big shock to me since as long as I remembered there had been hustling and bustling around the home with a lot of sibling play and rivalry. It was now quiet moments at dinner and other times during the day. No one spoke much. For some strange reason, I did not see why it was important to stay up late or to look forward to dinner, which was by far the most interesting part of our days.

After dinner, when Dad was alive, we would sit and chat about life, or he would scare us half to death with his stories. We would sit around him spellbound. His stories were a welcome treat and a break from our books. After he died, we went on without much to look forward to.

I would spend hours around the garden and house looking for things to do to occupy my time. I found the only thing I could do was read. We had many books, since my brothers and sisters had finished school and their books remained behind. I would read anything I could get my hands on: *Reader's Digest*, magazines, newspapers, novels, and anything that would occupy the time, even if it was not necessarily interesting.

Around February 1982, my sister Puchie was about to leave for the United States. This was the first time my best friend and I would be apart. All my life, no matter how messed up or confused things got, I had her. She made things better. When I had to face the reality of her leaving, I felt immense sadness. Like before, I kept it all in and said to myself it was for the best and I would not let it bother me. I was hopeful that someday we would all be together again, but I was indescribably sad and hurt. Nevertheless, Puchie left for the United States and I was left alone again.

I had about four months left to finish high school, and there was limited bus service to and from school from my home, so Mom sent me to my uncle's house some distance away. I moved in with my uncle and his two sons for a few months to finish off high school.

My life truly changed from this point forward. I moved to my uncle's in January 1982. My only goal was to complete high school and score the highest grade possible, and then join Puchie in the United States. My plan was to do this as soon as school was over. I focused on this goal. Mom instructed me to study, study, study, and nothing else.

As the youngest, I wanted to fend for myself and not depend on my brothers and sisters. I wanted my independence. My mom was busy working to provide resources to send me to school. During her childhood days, it was customary not to educate daughters. They were married off, sometimes as young as fourteen. Mom had regrets of not going to school. She is still unable to read or write. However, she was determined to have her children go to school.

The days grew longer. School dragged on with a lot of extra work needed to prepare for final examinations. We would study all day and stay later in school to complete extra practice exams. I was determined to do one thing: finish school and pass the final examinations. I stayed on course and never let anything get in the way.

But I was fifteen, and the hormones were definitely kicking in. For the first time, I started to think about boys. Some days that was all I thought of. Before then, a boy could have walked naked in front of me and I could not have cared less. Now, I found myself checking out the boys! What a surprise.

Months went by, and April 1982 finally came. We were ready to take final examinations. I felt I was prepared. However, I did have a big distraction between January and April. I fell in love. You could call it big, right? Well, you may be asking yourself, how could it happen? All she was doing was going to school and studying. Wrong! Let me tell you my simple story, but first, let me walk you through some of the basic concepts of our traditional beliefs. They may help you understand my story as it unfolds.

Education and culture have been extremely important for my success. These have a common element: discipline of the mind and senses. Therefore, I must at every stage of life pay close attention to them.

Dreams of All Young Girls

Culture and tradition form pathways in the journey of life.

The time toward the end of secondary school, the equivalent of a US high school, is the time in a young person's life when we begin to plan and formulate our future and how that future will be defined. In Guyana, a person generally completes secondary school between the ages of fifteen and seventeen. I used that time wisely to make decisions with regard to my future. First, I wanted to relocate to the United States, primarily to improve the quality of my life, as the economic conditions of beautiful Guyana had deteriorated rapidly over the years. It was close to impossible for a young girl to go off to the only reputable university, University of Guyana, in the capital city of Georgetown. Parents did not allow their daughters to go off to boarding school at that time, and I was sure my mom would not have allowed me to go off to university. Being born last, I felt very sheltered growing up. I felt I would not get my independence much like my older siblings. Nevertheless, I was confident I was not going to end my education with secondary school.

At the same time, I wanted to ensure I maintained my traditional values of being a kind, loving, and caring individual. In addition, my cultural expectations of being an obedient daughter and loyal wife were not going to change. I had to preserve these values at all cost. Furthermore, the process of dating and getting to know a person before making a decision on marriage was unacceptable at that time. Generally, there were more arranged marriages than marriages resulting from dating. In most cases, there was no intimacy before marriage.

Marriage was a lifetime commitment, and divorce was unheard of. It was not the means to end a marriage. Sadly, suicide was the primary solution, probably even a more acceptable one. truthWorse yet, most acceptable was to remain in a broken marriage and not let anyone know the marriage was broken. There was no professional counseling available to anyone in any capacity. Today, living in a free world, counseling is widely available; however, those in my culture underutilize it. I think people view it as a weakness, as it demonstrates a break from the traditional values of not letting others know about our private lives.

I used to see the wives in my neighborhood continuously experiencing abuse, both physical and verbal. I used to listen to the arguments and swearing, generally late at night, when husbands came home after hours of drinking. At times, the abuse would extend to the children as well. I witnessed numerous beatings; children were told not to talk back, or more beatings resulted. Looking back now, I definitely grew up in a sheltered home. I did not witness abuse or drinking in my home. Since my dad was disabled, he was not in a physical condition to move or even argue without getting exhausted. My older siblings told me he used to drink and sometimes argue with my mom. However, I never witnessed any of it. My childhood home was safe from abuse, alcohol, and harm.

My older siblings took good care of me. My dad ensured I was safe from harm. My mom ensured I was well fed and educated. Hence, I had the fuel I needed to lead a successful life. I planned to fully embrace those privileges and use them to plan and define my future. Fortunately, I did not have to think about that for a very, very long time to come.

I believe that by adhering to our culture, we create and sustain a society regulated by moral values, order, peace, and happiness.

The One

I am amazed as to the mysterious ways of love.

It was late January 1982, days after I moved to my uncle's house. I was enjoying a nice sunny afternoon. My two cousins were both working in the garden behind the house. I was looking at them from a seated position while reading a magazine. We were chitchatting when suddenly a tall, dark, and handsome guy walked past my window and went straight to my cousins. He did not see me. I looked at him for a while as he chatted with them. He was saying something funny because I heard a burst of laughter.

"What's so funny?" I asked out of curiosity.

This guy turned around and looked in the general direction of the kitchen window. What a handsome face he had! I was about to shyly escape into the house, but I couldn't as he started walking to the window. I felt motionless and numb. My heart was about to explode.

He came bravely up to me and said, "Robbie here," as he extended his hand to me. I said to myself, *How nice of him, not to mention, how cute.* I stared into those dark brown eyes and fell in love. I said to myself, *This is the one.* I knew it and was sure of it. I was only fifteen, but who cares. It was love at first sight.

To be honest with you, I really could not remember what happened after that. The only thing I remember is that I did not sleep that night. I was finally bitten by the "love bug." I kept seeing Robbie's face and wondering who he was. This was a mystery guy. Of course, I learned later on, he was one popular guy and well known with the girls. I also heard he was a bad boy and a rebel. Yes, at fifteen that was attractive.

From the first day on, he kept popping in every evening to chat with my cousins. This went on for weeks. I watched out for him but never talked much. That changed one early morning.

The school bus came around 7:30 a.m. each day. I would get up early to help my cousins fix breakfast and then get ready for school. I walked to the road in front of the house and waited for the bus each morning. I always had a book to read while waiting. Suddenly, out of nowhere, Robbie came up to me with an odd look on his face.

"How are you?" he said.

"OK," I replied.

"I guess the bus is late today."

"I don't think so."

He ran out of small talk. I was anxious to get rid of him, as much as he did not want to leave. I waited another few minutes, then said,

"I think you need to leave." Being blunt and assertive obviously was not an issue for me even at fifteen.

"Why?" he asked.

"Well, it does not look good with me standing here talking to you," I replied.

"So? We're talking," he said.

"Yes, but that's not what people might say," I insisted.

"Well, I'm staying until the bus comes," he declared.

Suddenly, the bus came and I got on. *What's the issue with this boy? I wondered. Is he dumb or something? Why couldn't he leave? He can't possibly know I have a crush on him!*

This went on for weeks. Each morning we went through the same routine. Robbie got braver and braver by the minute, and I kept telling him to bug off over and over again, but he became more persistent. Half the time he talked and I stared into space. The morning was not enough. He started to wait for me in the afternoon when the bus came home! God, what had I done to deserve this? I was embarrassed and definitely did not know how to handle strong emotions well. I started "sweating" from the minute I got up in the mornings until I boarded the bus and then again in the evenings when I got off the bus until I reached the house.

Finally, his persistent behavior paid off. One morning he did not come to wait with me. I kept looking and looking in the general direction of his house, but to no avail. I was mad at him for not coming!

After school that day, I came off the bus and he wasn't there. I went home. He did not visit that day either. That night I couldn't sleep. I wanted him revert to his normal and annoying routine of standing and saying nothing while I waited for the bus, ignoring him.

The next morning I was relieved to see him. I wanted to ask where he was the day before, but I kept my mouth firmly shut. Not even a smile. He should pay for not showing up one day. Who did he think he was? I did not have all day to waste with him and to think about him. Well, it's easy to talk big. After a lifelong minute, the conversation began as usual.

"Where were you yesterday?" I asked, not so nicely.

"You missed me?" he sneered.

"What? You must be joking."

"I got in trouble with my dad. He says I am always gone and not helping. So I had to go work with them yesterday all day. We got back late and I was too tired to wait for you."

"Oh, you don't have to wait for me. I'm fine," I corrected.

I was relieved; at least he was doing something good at home. For the first time in weeks, we started to have normal conversations. The one thing I liked about him was that it was easy to have a conversation. He did not always agree with me but had opinions of his own. I found this attractive and engaging. He would not just agree with me like most of my other friends. He stood his ground well. I respected him more.

Months went by, and I was having feelings I never had before. I was thinking of him and watching out for him. He looked at me with tenderness and love. I must have reciprocated, because he kept coming each day, any chance he would get.

Sadly, all good things must come to an end. It was around April 1982 and time for final exams. My plans were to leave my uncle's house go home by the end of exams. The last week was solemn. Robbie and I did not talk much. I knew I was going to miss him, and I was sure he was going to be sad. When the week ended, he came for his last visit with me. He was almost in tears, and so was I. He asked when he was going to see me again, and I said I did not know. He said he would come to visit me at my home.

"You have got to be kidding!" I exclaimed.

"No, seriously, I will come," he replied.

"But I live so far away. How will you get there, and when you do, what will you tell my mom?" I asked.

"I don't know, but I will come," he insisted.

"I'll miss you and your stupid questions," I said without thinking.

He got up, took my hand, and said, "Don't forget me."

He left. I cried.

Exams were over and I was relieved. For the first time since I could remember, I did not have any studying to do. Freedom, what a relief! What would I do? Not to worry, my mom always found something for me to do since she believed there was a risk of us daughters running off with some boy and causing disgrace to the family. Not to mention we might even have intimacy, and God knows how that would look! I knew boredom would not be mine. I had books to read and lots and lots of notepads on which to write all my thoughts and feeling. Yes, boredom was not mine.

By May 1982, I was back home and missing school, my friends, and of course, the boy I'd fallen for. I found myself thinking of him continuously and wished I were back with him shooting the breeze, sharing crazy stories that made no sense. I missed the silly humor and laughs. I was hopeful Robbie would come to visit as promised, but the summer came and went, and he never came by. I was enjoying my old neighborhood friends, whom I was not able to do much with during my dad's long years of illness. I loved hanging around the house with them and doing what kids do in the summer, having fun.

Lakhram lived next door with his wife and his daughter, Kunti. I spent a lot of my time playing with her. My mom was busy trying to find boys to marry me. At that time, when a young lady finished secondary school, the next step was to prepare her for marriage. Mom would come home from her trips and tell me about how she'd talked to this friend who had promised to come with her husband to "scope" me out for their son. But no one ever came to scope me out. Arranged marriages were the norm back then.

I was way too busy daydreaming about Robbie. I listened to my mom and nodded my head, but I knew that no one would tell me whom or when to marry. This was definitely not an acceptable attitude in our culture. Parents were supposed to find a suitable match for each of us. Eventually, my mom gave up on me. I felt she knew all along I was more independent than my siblings. She knew my dad was partly to blame for some of it. Finally, she made a decision: she decided I was responsible enough to join my other siblings in the United States.

An older sister from my dad's first marriage, Uma, lived in Canada. My mom said I could go there to stay with her for a while. She arranged for me to fly into Canada. At some point, my final destination would be the United State, but only after assisting my sister with some baby-sitting. It worked out well. Within a year of completing school, I went to Canada, and a few months helped me get to know my older sister and her family. In July of 1983, I left Canada for New York City. I was then sixteen years old.

I left Guyana with a pain in my heart. I liked it there. Home had been a happy place for me. I had many friends after my dad died, and even a boyfriend. I saw Robbie the day before I left. I went for a weekend to visit my uncle and cousins where I met Robbie, and I asked my cousin to let Robbie know I was visiting. Robbie came and we were able to talk for a few minutes. I was sad. We said our good-byes and went our own ways. It was difficult, but it needed to be done. My life was going in a different direction.

My emotions were ones I had never experienced before. I tried to ignore them, but eventually I learned I had to heed and deal with them. This was an all-new experience. I tried to plan for the future, but strong emotional feelings tended to dilute my plans by taking away much-needed focus.

I am not afraid to take calculated, well-thought-out risks in life. They can turn out to be pathways to different experiences and environments that are crucial for growth.

Life in the Big City

*Make yourself busy doing what you
like, and time fades away.*

Life in the United States was fast and furious. I expected the apartment my brother, sister, and nephew shared to be luxurious, but it was clearly on the other end of the spectrum. The apartment was in Long Island City, Queens, New York, a few blocks from the East River that separates the boroughs of Queens and Manhattan. We were on the third floor with no elevator and little to no heat. Roaches thought it was their apartment. It took a lot from me to look at the positive side because there was no positive side I could see, other than reconnecting with my sister Puchie. Nonetheless, it was home for us: Puchie, Shammie, my nephew Vic, and me. Vic's mom is one of my older half sisters from my Dad's first marriage. Vic was working and attending a university in New York.

We continued to live in the one-bedroom apartment for a couple of years. The the bathroom had room for one person, standing room only. You either turned around slowly or bumped and fell. There were no closets. One full and one twin bed stood wall-to-wall in the only bedroom with no room for anything else. By now, we were becoming used to the area. We were able to purchase food and supplies at some of the more inexpensive shops and stores. We were surviving and planning our future.

We became a tight bunch. We immediately dove into what we came to do: work and go back to school. This was the American dream for most immigrants. I did not need to go to high school in New York City, so I studied for my GED and passed it. I was seventeen. I had to work and pay one-fourth of all shared expenses, including rent. My urge to succeed and be independent was overwhelming.

My first job was at an American Greetings card shop in the Empire State Building. I started packing cards and helping customers. From here came my sense of customer service and learning that the customer is always right. After a few months, I was promoted to cashier. My hourly pay was now a whopping $3.50 per hour! My wage was about $150 per week. Hey, this was a lot of money for a seventeen-year-old. From the $600 a month I earned, I had to pay around $150 in rent, $75 for groceries, and $20 in train tokens. This left me with enough spending money. It was not a lot of money. I opened a bank account and started a saving account. I was learning to manage my own account and save money. This lesson would definitely come in handy later in my life as well.

Working in the city was a dream. I had access to the great bookstores, libraries, and parks, especially Central Park. I was truly at peace and definitely found serenity there.

Was it really that bad? No, living there was the best time of our lives. We were a bunch of kids living and learning how to manage our bills and save money while enjoying life. Even though it was tough, we lived happily together.

We each worked two jobs to make ends meet. I had a journal where I kept a log of how much I made and how much I spent. I had a goal each month to save a forecasted amount. Meeting my forecast, satisfied me that I was managing my finances well. Looking back, life was great for the four of us. We were kids having fun and not worrying about anything. I wish at some level that our lives had not changed, but life changes all of us at some time or another.

I had been the last one to come to the United States, so there was a little adjustment period where I had to learn the culture and adapt to a more Western lifestyle. I considered myself an introvert, and I was happy being by myself or with small groups. In the beginning, I avoided the malls or anywhere there was a large crowd. However, I believe humans are highly adaptable, and I found I was becoming more social and outgoing. It took a few months, but I started to go out socially, primarily dancing. Finally, I felt my social skills were starting to develop in a more mature way. I felt depressed at times from having that much responsibility at a young age, but I had my family around me to make it better. They made all the difference in the world.

I was starting to write letters to Robbie back in Guyana telling him about my new life. I wrote him several letters but did not get any response. I was starting to think he was over me. It was painful not to get a letter.

I dated a lot from about seventeen to twenty. I made some good choices and some not-so-good choices. As I recall, there were about five guys I dated. I always compared each one with Robbie, but I did not feel anything close to what I felt for him. He was still the one. Nevertheless, I enjoyed dating, the dinners, the movies, the fun, and laughs that came with dating. They were great times that led to some level of emotional maturity, and I think everyone should have an opportunity to experience this.

Shammie purchased his first home in Corona, Queens, sometime in 1984. It was a memorable year for us. We were finally going to get out of the hideous apartment. I believe it was late spring or early summer of 1984 when we moved into the home. It was a trek to the train station, but we did not care. We had a backyard, three bedrooms, a basement, and a large kitchen. Puchie and I shared a room, and Vic finally had a bed in his own room! I was sure he was happy after sleeping on a sofa in the apartment for three years! Shammie had a room of his own as well. We were happy and looking forward for the years ahead to live happily ever after.

Wait a minute—you're probably thinking it's too soon for the happily ever after, right? No, I want you to know my happily ever after was here. I did not know it then, but years later, I realized that I would have given anything to go back to this time. This was it. I was happy up until this point in my adult life—truly, innocently happy.

I have established clear and defined values by which I will live my life. Temptations will be there to sway me off course. When they come, I try my best to stay the course. If I fail, I will get up and get right back on course. I will make mistakes and say or do the wrong things, but I will try to learn from them.

Living Life on Life's Terms

Things that are destined to happen will happen.

Nineteen eighty-five was a memorable year. Shammie was preparing to get married, and Puchie was going back to Guyana to get married. Love was all around us. Our lives were starting to enter a new phase.

I recalled what my dad used to say to us during those nights of storytelling. He said to make sure to marry a person who loved us more. His reasoning; we had a better chance of that person taking care of and making sacrifices and compromises for us. He was also sure the marriage would have a better chance of being a happy one. He also knew we were a loving and caring family of caregivers and was sure we would grow up to be loving and caring partners without being controversial or judgmental of others. I believed he did not want anyone to take advantage of our kindness.

I finally received a letter from Robbie! His first letter was wonderful to read. We continued to correspond. He asked when I was going back to visit him and declared he was looking forward to spending the rest of his life with me. We stayed in touch from that point on. In addition, I finally got to meet his eldest brother and wife, Ramchand and Baby. They were already living in New York and were only a short train ride from where we lived.

I was beside myself with joy. I again started to dream the dream of all little girls, except I was not so little anymore. I was close to twenty years old and had grown more responsible and emotionally mature.

It is traditional for the parents of the groom to request the bride's hand in marriage. I asked Robbie to let his parents know they would have to ask my mom for my hand in marriage. My mom was bent on an arranged marriage for me, but she knew I would not comply, especially in choosing a life partner. Finally, she agreed for me to marry Robbie, but not before letting me know it would never work out. She made sure I heard it.

"You are not the same. You will struggle. He did not go to school as much as you. I heard he is a 'bad boy.' I heard he has girlfriends everywhere. He will leave you or hurt you," my mom advised.

What did she know? She was wrong. Love was the best thing in life. It was simple, pure, and unconditional. To this day mom's words still rings in my ears.

Shammie got married in June 1986. He and his beautiful new bride moved into the Corona home he owned. Puchie and I were still living there. A few months following the wedding, Puchie and I decided to leave and find an apartment. I was almost twenty and Puchie was twenty-two. We did not have an abundance of money, but we both worked. We had no idea what living would cost.

Puchie reminded me as I was writing this book how confused she was. We were clueless as to where we would go. I remembered we sat on a bench by the train station for hours, planning and organizing our thoughts. Finally, we came up with a plan.

In our quest for a new place to live, Puchie and I went to my cousin Kamal's house first. We did not have to go anywhere else. She had an attic she was not using, an open studio. We asked her if we could stay there for a while until we saved up some money for an apartment. She and her husband agreed immediately. I will never forget her generosity and extreme kindness. She will forever be blessed. We moved into our first place that summer of 1986.

We bought some comforters and a mattress. We had a small stove and a small refrigerator. We made ourselves a home, though Puchie and I both worked two jobs and were rarely home. When I was home, I would take my bicycle to the parks and spend all day reading and riding around.

I needed to save up a lot of money to cover expenses to go back to Guyana. My sense of discipline with money was phenomenal. I did not spend money on unnecessary junk. I made sure I ate well, stayed healthy, and wore decent clothes, but I did not go out often to eat. We learned to cook a lot and I found I really enjoyed it.

In the fall of 1986, Puchie found out her husband was coming from Guyana. We knew we had to get a real apartment with privacy, so started looking, and finally found one two blocks from the train station, a small, two-bedroom apartment with a mini kitchen and a small living room. We signed the papers and moved into the apartment in December of 1986. Puchie's husband arrived the week of Christmas 1986, and incidentally, I left for Guyana that week to see Robbie. Life was moving ahead swiftly for us all.

When I am in need, I now know I should ask for help. Many people derive great happiness from helping others. I know if I do not ask for help, no one will know I need help. I must reach out, without pride or egoism.

Life's New Experiences

*Think well before you speak or act, and
don't ignore your gut feelings.*

I'd left Guyana in 1983, and it was now December 1986. I was twenty years old. A lot had happened in that span of time. I knew the man I loved and was going to marry. I knew my life would continue to be pulled apart from my siblings as each got married. I was nervous and happy at the same time, but life's changes are inevitable.

A few weeks prior to my trip, Robbie was involved in an accident. He was thrown from a car going about eighty miles an hour and almost lost his life. He was still recovering when I made the trip. I was worried about how he was feeling and whether my visiting would be too much pressure. We talked on the phone, and he assured me he was fine, he loved me, and he could not wait to see me. I echoed the same feelings. I was on top of the world at that moment. I felt love as I had never felt it before. It was the greatest feeling in the world. I never want to live my life without that feeling. I would fight to keep the feeling of love in my heart. I was sure of this.

The day I boarded the plane to go back home, I knew it was going to be a long flight, at least five hours. For the first time I started to think about the person I was going to marry and what life would be like with him. I was scared and uncertain about the whole idea of getting married. I remembered what everyone told me about Robbie and his popularity with the girls. I loved him, but what if he did not love me back? I started to feel a strong sense of doubt. I had never felt this unsure before. What was going on in my creative mind? Was there something I should look at before making this lifelong commitment?

At one point in the flight, I was hoping the plane would turn around and go back to the life in New York I had grown accustomed to. I did not want to go to Guyana or marry anyone at such a young age. How could

I feel that way? I loved Robbie. I should have felt elated and self-assured. Nevertheless, I felt what I was feeling, and it was not going away.

I was drunk by the time we landed. I could not get my brain to stop analyzing, so I needed something to take the edge off and drank on the plane. I'd never done this before—a spontaneous, irresponsible act of letting it all go. It felt really good. Alcohol sure helped me stop thinking.

Was something happening that I did not know of? Did my inner self or subconscious know something my conscious mind did not know? If this were the case, I would surely find out in time. Only God knew the future, and he would protect me from any bad decisions I was innocently about to make. I was ready to face anything that came my way.

I realize now that drinking never solved my problem. How could it? It impairs the mind, fogs the senses, and diminishes other normal functions. Admittedly, there is a feeling of elation, but once I come back to earth, I still need to deal with my issues and fears.

Dog Days of Heaven

True love does exist; we have to keep our eyes open.

It took nearly two long hours to clear the Guyana Customs and Immigration. The process was extremely slow. I had to remind myself to keep my mouth shut. This was not a place I would want to express my honest opinion, as it could earn me the privilege of having to wait even longer. The temperature felt like it was over one hundred degrees with the humidity factor was equally high. At that time there was no air-conditioning system. It took another two hours or so to get my bags. In the meantime, I was wondering what it would be like when I saw Robbie. Would I feel happiness, joy, or elation? How would I feel? At that point, I wanted to turn around and run in the opposite direction. Run anywhere, just run.

Eventually, I came out to the passenger waiting area with some help from a baggage handler. I saw Robbie for the first time in three long years. He was extremely skinny and pale. He had huge scars on this face and looked like he was going to faint. It was a result of the car accident where the vehicle rolled over several times and the passengers, Robbie among them, were tossed out. I later learned the accident resulted from drinking and driving.

Robbie walked up to me and hugged me. One hug and I felt the love again instantly. I knew I loved him and that the feeling in the plane was temporary fear, which faded away instantly. We held each other for a long time. How could I feel so much love for another person? Matters of the heart were pure, and I was on a high and unconditionally in love. I felt we were bound together forever. I felt it in my heart. Robbie was the one. I knew it. I was sure he felt the same, no matter what anyone said to me in the past about his being the "bad boy" of the neighborhood. He loved me for me and wanted only me. At that moment, it was all that mattered. He did not care about anything else but me. I was happy.

Being this close to someone I loved was the best feeling I'd experienced in my life. I believe in the joys of pure love and it being an unselfish gift. I wished to cherish the moments forever. There was no other feeling like it in the world. It was pure, it was honest, and it was truly mind blowing. It was unconditional. I was loved.

We spent that night in the airport's waiting area along with our driver and decided to drive home at dawn because the last ferry had already departed. Early the next morning, the driver, Robbie, and I left to take the ferry, known as Torani, across the Berbice River, which separates our region from the capital city of Georgetown where the airport is located. We arrived at the ferry station and had to wait awhile for the first ferry run of the day. It generally comes around 5:00 a.m. to facilitate the business travelers. The ferry carried passengers as well as dozens of cars, trucks, and buses. It was amazing to see this old vessel chugging its way slowing across the river toward us. I remembered how as a child I used to love looking at this majestic vessel. Looking at it now was like reliving my childhood.

The ferry came and we boarded slowly, one car at a time. I was starting to remember the familiar sights in Guyana. I had been gone so long, I had forgotten a lot and was amazed by the beauty of the country I was born in. I was finally starting to remember the places and how I used to love going to school in one of the main towns, New Amsterdam. The ports were the same, the bus station was dilapidated, and the businesses around the area were mostly closed down, but the people were still the same. The ferry finally reached the other side and we disembarked.

The first stop on our trip from the airport was 45 Village at Robbie's home. As we drove from the dockside, we passed famous landmarks such as the sprawling and tranquil cane fields in Palmyra. We passed the hustling and bustling town of Rose Hall with the quaint shops, cafes, and markets. We proceeded to pass the two largest movie theaters, Apollo and Roopmahal. These were all famous landmarks in my province where I used to wander around as a child, chaperoned by older siblings.

Next, we entered one of the oldest communities where my family was born, 45 Village, my final destination for that day. It was the day after Christmas in 1986. As we drove toward Robbie's house, I saw the home my dad owned before we relocated to the farming community of Black Bush Polder. There stood the home where most of my siblings were born.

The yard was overgrown with brush, and the fruit trees were standing tall and needed some trimming. The home was old and literally falling apart. I felt sad to see this home had lost its character and glory. I closed my eyes and tried to imagine what it must have looked like with my older siblings running around gleefully.

I was extremely tired from the long trip. I met Robbie's parents, his two nieces, his sister, and his younger brother, Kumar, whom I knew from high school. Finally, it was nice to meet the people I would be family with for the rest of my life. They were kind. We went upstairs to Robbie's room, and I took a long, much-needed nap. I was dead tired from the trip.

The next day I spent with Robbie's family trying to get to know them. It was a pleasure to get to meet and know his wonderful parents, his only sister, and her family. I felt welcomed, respected, and appreciated by his family. I was starting to relax and live for the moment. I no longer was on edge. I no longer had apprehension. I no longer had fears.

I strongly believe cultural trends control our behaviors to a great extent. I should respect and abide by them, as they are important in regulating my behaviors to reflect moral order.

Good Riddance

Return we must to the life we have built for ourselves.

My week in Guyana was fun, yet relaxing. This is the Caribbean. The stillness of life, the beauty of nature, and the vastness of the beaches were enough to make a person not want to leave.

We visited Robbie's extended family and some close friends. I was enjoying and absorbing it all. We visited my home where I grew up, the home where I was with my dad. Mom was there at the time of my visit, and she was extremely happy to see me happy.

As I approached my home, fond memories came to life. The memories I shared with my other siblings and my parents. The family balcony we used to gather on. From a distance, I imagined my dad sitting and waiting for me. He would have been proud of me. I was sure of this as I entered the main gate of this majestic home. The paint was peeling off, there were a few scattered flowers, and the yard needed much more care. It saddened me to see this structure looking lonely and neglected. I spent an entire day wandering around and absorbing all that was around me. Home would always be home, no matter that I had moved away.

I was in Guyana for only a week. I spent part of my time at Robbie's home and the rest of the time visiting relatives and friends. It was a short visit, but I made the most of the days and tried to reconnect with my roots and my childhood. Even though I had grown up, I still had appreciation for the life I had and the nature that surrounded it.

Finally, the days in Guyana came to an end. I was preparing for my long journey back to the United States. Robbie and I were both sad, and he did not know what to do or say. We both were unsure when we would see each other again. The pain of separation was deep for both of us. I was able to share those feeling with him; however, Robbie was not much of a talker, and I felt he was not able to share how he felt. I assumed we both felt the same.

I would eventually learn that open communication is vital to the success of a relationship and the lack of it could destroy a potentially good relationship. It is important that we learn how to talk amicably and clearly express our feelings. This is a skill that can be learned over time. I learned it and continue to learn. People make grave assumptions if they do not know what we are thinking or feeling. I now know love is not the only key ingredient in a good relationship. It takes understanding and respecting each other, communicating with each other, and protecting each other from harm and pain.

The plane trip back was long and tiresome. We stopped in Trinidad and took another plane to New York City. Finally, after several hours, I reached home where my brother, sister, and nephew awaited me.

I believe a person will have greater respect for me and hold me in high esteem if I stick to my core values and adhere to them during trying times. I promise myself I will stand up for what I believe in, even if at the end of the day I am left standing alone. I am in good company.

Start of a Union

Habits are easy to form but difficult to break.

Early in 1987, Robbie came to the United States. I was excited beyond description. I wanted us to get married and live happily ever after. We would have the perfect life. Never once did I consider that he might not love me as much in return. I went with my heart and allowed myself to live with the joys that followed. It was a decision I never regretted, but it was also a decision that made me view love and those I would love differently in future years.

When Robbie came, he moved in with me. My family did not object, but it weighed heavily on my conscience. I convinced myself it was all right to move in together and start our lives while the wedding plans were underway. I deliberately went against my cultural beliefs. I knew I would have to take responsibility for those actions, and I do. At that time, I did not have the experience or the maturity to separate my emotions from my actions. I now know those come with experience. I am now able to make that separation.

Robbie and I immediately started to plan the wedding set for that same year. Well, let me stand corrected—I immediately started to plan the wedding. Robbie was not offering to help. He was busy meeting up with his long lost friends and hanging out, drinking, and having a ball. In the meantime, I was exhausted going shopping and preparing for the wedding.

I would get home, and Robbie would not be there. No phone calls. No communication. Eventually, he would either show up alone, drunk, or with some friends. He introduced me as the girl he was going to marry, but I was starting to feel like a trophy sitting on his mantel and not the person he loved. This continued until I told him to stop displaying me and to come home on time. He did for a few weeks and then reverted to old habits repeatedly.

I was starting to wonder whether we were going to be able to make a life together. Each time I confronted Robbie, he would say he was sorry and that he loved me. This behavior was consistent and kept happening every other week or so. I felt like I was going crazy and running out of options. In the meantime, I was working on getting the wedding plans together. I was really getting frustrated.

It was the beginning of summer in 1987. We were ready to perform the legal marriage ceremony at City Hall in New York City. On June 21, 1987, we were legally wed. We made the decision to perform the legal ceremony so that Robbie could obtain his permanent legal status in the United States. In the meantime, we were still preparing for the religious ceremony later that year.

Puchie was the only witness at our ceremony at City Hall. I remember asking Robbie to wear a dress shirt and tie. You would have thought I had asked him to cut out his right lung and give it to me! He was arguing and swearing he would not wear a tie to get married. This, on the morning of the most wonderful day of our lives! He ended up wearing the tie, but he was mad all the way there and during the ceremony. As soon as the ceremony was over, he angrily took the tie off.

I sat quietly on the train ride back from the ceremony, wondering if this was how my life would be each day. I wondered how someone I loved so much could care so little about how I felt. I was too young and naïve to understand that these were early signs of a potentially troubled relationship. I was starting to learn a lot about what the rest of my life was going to be. At that time, I was sure he would change as he became older or better yet I would love him unconditionally and he would change as a result of it.

I think it's wise to address issues as soon as they surface. Delay in doing so can cause an escalation. Not addressing issues prevented me from unveiling other related behaviors affecting the relationship.

Leaping into Life

When in doubt, follow your heart.

The months went by quickly from June to August. I was shopping a lot with my mom to prepare for the wedding in October. She was visiting the United States that summer and was a tremendous help to me in planning my wedding. Imagine going shopping with your mom, who would prefer you wear a red sari. You see, in my mind a red sari would imply I was a virgin, but we now know this was not the case. I had long since had intimacy, and it would be an insult to wear red, at least in my mind. My mother knew, but she insisted I wear red because it would look bad if people inferred I was not a virgin. It was all about what "our people" might think. Living up to everyone else's expectations but our own was a norm I grew up with.

I really did not care what people thought about me but my mom did. I was starting to carve my own path as I had in my childhood years. I was starting to build great confidence in myself by just being me. Mom had very little influence on my decision. I purchased a yellow sari.

The summer of 1987 was fun for Robbie. He would work, go drinking after work, and come home later and later. We went to the movies a few times after I complained. Was this the life I really wanted? I wanted someone to be there with me cooking dinner, going for a walk, reading or watching TV, and having conversations. Robbie was not up for any of that nonsense. It was the beginning of loneliness, and I was not twenty-one years old yet. I was sure that this was the life I would hate. I was much too happy as a person to settle for feeling alone and unloved. I felt unappreciated. I felt I wanted out of the relationship.

In August 1987, I made a decision. I decided I was not going to stay married to Robbie. I planned to cancel the religious ceremony scheduled to take place in October. I simply changed my mind. I had it all planned. We would split the cash we had in the bank. This was a whopping $1,600. I would let Robbie know I still loved him, but I planned to tell him we were two different and incompatible individuals. Even though we might love each other, we would not be able to have a good life together as husband and wife. He did not want to be tied down or commit to anyone. I wanted to be married and was willing to give up the rest of my single life and be with him as my partner for life, but I felt he was unwilling to make the same sacrifices. It was my grand exit plan.

On a Saturday morning, I woke up early and asked Robbie to listen to what I had to say. We were both in our bedroom. My sister and her husband were still asleep in the other room. I spoke as softly as I could. At twenty years old, there was no life experience for me to draw from. I was unsure how to articulate my feelings and sad at the same time. However, I was able to get through what I had to say. I handed Robbie a check for eight hundred dollars and told him it represented half of what we had in the bank. He did not say one word. He just sat there. I thought it was a great way to end a relationship. He was happy to be able to move on with his life and not be burdened by the demands of a wife—a wife he apparently did not care to do anything with or for. He took the check and left. I was finally breathing normally again, but I spent most of the remaining morning in tears. The pain and hurt were immense; nevertheless, I knew I'd done the right thing. Ending it then would be a lot less painful than if I had to end it later.

That evening my mother came back with Robbie to talk to me. Robbie had gone to my family and told them I'd stopped the wedding and ended the marriage. This did not sit well with my family. I had a lot to think about, they said. I was ending a marriage with a perfectly good guy who was in love with me. I should be ashamed, they said. The pressure to go through with the ceremony was building.

I did not tell my family that Robbie was not the person I wanted to spend the rest of my life with and that I had possibly made a mistake in judgment. I did not tell them he was gone all the time and spent little to no time with me. I did not tell them that every day he came home from work drunk. Why did I not tell them? I did not tell them he would order me not to go over to Shammie's house or would refuse to go with me. I had no problems talking to my family. I realize now that experience and confidence in oneself do not come easily and certainly did not come at the ripe age of twenty. I had to learn these and other skills as I grew older. I should have listened to my mother from the beginning when she told me not to marry Robbie. She was right.

I was confused now because my mom was telling me he was a "good guy." Given my cultural values, sleeping with a person once is considered taboo if you do not marry the person. At the time, I was sure no other guy would want to marry me or even consider marrying me because I had already slept with another person. That was then, this is now. I think differently now. I now know it is OK to have an intimate relationship with a person and still leave that relationship if there are clear signs it would not work out. I now know I have the power to change my mind.

I know the decision I'd made to leave Robbie was the right decision. Nevertheless, I gave in even though I was the most legitimate person to make decisions relating to my life. Elders may have opinions, and we may consider them, but at the end of the day, we have to decide for ourselves. We should consider advice from our parents, but in the end, we are the ones that should ultimately make a decision that is right for us as long as we know we are the ones to bear the consequences of our decisions. Nevertheless, I listened to everyone—and yes, I felt they knew what was best for me at that time. They were older and wiser. I decided to go through with the wedding. I decided to sacrifice the rest of my life and marry Robbie. I decided I would make it work at any cost.

I had carefully thought out the solution to my problem and was convinced I had made a correct decision. I should have stood by my original decision. I was the one who had to live with the consequences of changing my mind.

The Wedding

And the name of "spirit" was given to alcohol.

OK, after all the mental debate, you are probably wondering why I would get married to a guy like this when we were so different. Well, opposites attract, and yes, I was in love with him and was fully committed to this relationship. I knew I would make it work, and I believed he loved me. How could I make this turnaround so quickly? Age, experience and emotional maturing was probably not a factor I considered back then, but life experiences becomes learning and teaching tools. At a very young age we make decisions more on emotions and not emotions combined with common sense or reality.

In the weeks following our brief breakup, Robbie's behavior improved dramatically. He might not have known how to show love, but he was more engaged with me. I also believed that most of the guys who grew up in our culture did not know or were not taught to express and show love and care. As a loyal Indian wife, it was customary to accept these shortcomings and know whatever the husband did, he really meant well. I told myself this, and I went on to believe it for many, many years to follow. I also knew that when I made a commitment to do something I would see it through to the end, even if it meant displacing myself and sacrificing my happiness. I was willing to make this sacrifice for the promises I made.

The wedding plans were completed, and all the food, saris, and other wedding necessities were purchased. The date was set for October 3, 1987. The pundit approved the date as an auspicious day for a wedding. Ironically, he did not approve us getting married. He said Robbie and I were like fire and oil, according to our sacred book. Based upon our characteristic traits, which are determined by the stars and planets under which we were born, we really did not match up. I felt he had no idea what he was talking about! Love could conquer anything. I knew in my heart that it was all that mattered. We would be married and live happily ever after long after that pundit died!

The big day came. The traditional activities were performed and well monitored by my mother. I went with the flow, having fun, and actually looking forward to the painfully long prayers needed to bless this wonderful day and the beautiful bride and groom. What I dreaded the most was the actual wedding ceremony. It is usually a long ceremony, sitting on the floor. You see, I wanted to ensure Robbie was not uncomfortable since he was complaining about sitting down too long. First, he did not want to wear the traditional Hindu garment men wore at their wedding. He was going to wear only white pants and a shirt or else he was not getting married. I gave in. He did not want to sit too long. Robbie wanted everything his way, and I made sure he had it. When he was happy, I was happy. At that time, it was exactly the way I felt. I behaved exactly the way I was taught to behave as a loyal wife, which I was determined to be. I figured most wives before me must have made the same sacrifices and they were able to remain in long-lasting, happy, relationships. I would do the same.

The ceremony went off without any problems, and soon it was time for the reception, the part I knew Robbie would enjoy. There was lots of food and alcohol. I thought this was the only part of the day he would truly enjoy, the drinking, and I was absolutely right.

My family had a surprise honeymoon planned for us. They had ordered a limousine and booked a two-night hotel stay at one of the nicer hotels on the waterfront off the Hudson River in Manhattan. They had our bags packed with all the necessities for two days. This was the greatest surprise I'd had so far in my life. Little did I know there was an even bigger surprise awaiting me.

Robbie refused to go on our honeymoon! Yes, he absolutely refused. He was irate that he had to leave his friends and the drinking and go off with me to a hotel in a limousine! He was raging with anger and wanted to start an argument with my family and me. I remembered feeling unloved at that moment, again! My husband refusing to go on our honeymoon! What on earth had I gotten myself into, and how was I ever going to endure this?

My emotions were racing in all directions. I was feeling hate, anger, resentment, regret, and many other emotions I had never felt before. Believe me, love was not one of the emotions. What did I do? Nothing. I told my family to tell the limousine driver to leave and to cancel the hotel room. I saw how unhappy it made Robbie, and I did not want him to be unhappy on this memorable day. I gave in again! Robbie was happy. He continued to drink and party. This was his honeymoon, spending his wedding night with his first love, alcohol!

I am now aware of my rights, and I insist I enjoy them. It doesn't matter who is involved, as long as no one gets hurt. I will not surrender my rights to anyone, even those who claim to love me.

The Lost Years

Stand up for what you believe is right.

Nineteen eighty-seven went by quickly. Robbie and I were starting to settle into married life. We were both working and saving money. Our goal—now I think it was my goal—was to save a lot of cash to purchase a home. At that time, I thought one needed around thirty thousand dollars for a down payment for a home in New York. I was making about $450 a week, and Robbie was making about $250. Since we shared the apartment with Puchie and her husband, we did not have many expenses. Our savings were rapidly climbing.

I do not really remember 1988 except the summer when my sister's husband died in Guyana. It was truly a sad occasion. Vic's father had passed away. I went with Vic to Guyana for the funeral. As I am writing this book, I recall it was the last time I visited my homeland. I really need to change that soon and take my children for a visit to the beautiful country I still love.

I stayed at Robbie's parents' house since they were a few miles from my sister's home and I did not want to burden my sister with staying at her home, as they were busy with planning and organizing the funeral. Robbie's parents were still living in Guyana at that time. I was there only a week or so. That was really all I remembered of the rest of 1987 and all of 1988. Did my new married life not made an imprint on my memory the first year? Or did I block out that year? I have no idea which one it is. There is so much I do not remember during the early years of my marriage. However, one other event made a permanent imprint on me.

One night soon after we were married, Robbie came home late and drunk long after I had gone to bed. This was starting to become a routine. I got up and asked him where he was. Out of nowhere, he slapped me with such force on the right side of my head that I flew across the bed. My head went backward, and I hit the iron heater on the other side of the bed against the window. It was the middle of the night, and Puchie and her husband were in the room next door, so I did not want to scream out, hence avoiding a confrontation with them. This was not one of the wisest decisions I made.

There was blood everywhere. I turned around, and the sheer white window draperies were splattered with a streak of blood. My pink nightgown was drenched with blood. I'm not sure if you have ever smelled the scent of fresh blood, but it is not a good smell. It is the scent of fear, in my opinion. I was experiencing intense fear for the first time in my life. I was afraid to utter another word in fear of the consequence.

This, I now know, was the start of an abusive relationship. Sadly, I did not know it then. I convinced myself that Robbie had hit me because I asked the wrong question. I strongly believed that I should not have asked him where he was. I felt I had made him angry. It was my fault. I was somewhat OK with his other behaviors—not going anywhere with me, the swearing or angry outbursts—but someone hitting me for the first time in my life was a big deal for me. I decided to ensure it never, ever happened again.

Robbie took me into the bathroom quietly and trimmed the hair around the wound and dressed it with God knows what. I was crying the whole time and could not stop shivering. I took off my nightgown, placed it in a garbage bag, and took it outside to the trash bin. I did not want anyone to know. I changed and went to bed. I remembered wanting to go to sleep and not wanting Robbie to even touch me.

The next morning, I woke him up. I clearly remember what I said.

"Don't you ever touch me again, as long as you live. Do not ever touch me again. I won't tell anyone this time, but if it ever happens again, I will ensure this marriage is completely over. Do not make me repeat myself."

He was shocked. He'd never seen me be this assertive before. I'd seemed to him a complete pushover, but I was not a pushover. I am, however, kind, loving, giving, and caring. This could be misconstrued as being too passive. Robbie made a tragic mistake. He mistook my kindness for my weakness. In fact, that kindness was my greatest strength. To this day, he has never touched me in anger again that I recall. Little did I know back then that physical abuse was not the only type of abuse that existed.

Puchie asked me the next morning why there were bloodstains on my nightgown. I was not sure how she had seen the stains, as I had changed, but I did not tell her the truth of what happened. I simply told her I had my period. I should have told her the truth. I should have told someone of the physical abuse. I should not have addressed it with Robbie. I wish I had known more about the behaviors of an abuser. I would have made better decisions.

As Puchie read the rough draft of my manuscript for the first time, she said she knew at the time I was probably lying about having a period. She was sad when she read this part of the book. She was sad for what I went through. She was sad because she should have probed further and not accepted my answer. She felt she may have also aided in denying that it was physical abuse. To this day, whenever I think of that night or retell the story, my right hand goes straight to my head, over two decades later.

I should have reached out for help when I was abused. Reaching out to my family, close friends, counselors, or to law enforcement would have made me more aware of domestic violence and abuse. I should have protected me and not my abuser.

Hello Florida

*Active alcoholics attract each other much
like moths to a blinding light.*

Early in 1989, Robbie and I visited the beautiful Sunshine State, Florida. This was our first trip anywhere. Robbie's cousins had moved there, and they were close. Well, I thought he was very close to me. Little did I know, these were his primary drinking buddies, and a special bond did existed. I learned a lot about Robbie based on whose company he kept as the years dragged on. Drinking buddies are like comfort food for an alcoholic. They reach out and cling to each other. I simply was second choice over friends and alcohol. Realizing that the only worth I had to my husband was funding his expenses was not a good feeling.

Still, this trip was a long-needed vacation. We were married going on two years, and I was happy we were at least going somewhere. I really did not care where I went as long as I got a short break from the mundane daily life I was starting to despise. Little did I know at that time that Robbie was planning to move to Florida. I would later learn that he planned ahead and knew what he wanted. He then manipulated and lied to get it.

But at this time I was happy to go anywhere with him, so I got immersed in the vacation and being in the sunshine away from the snow in New York. I fell for the manipulation hook, line, and sinker! During our weeklong vacation, Robbie and I started to look at homes with a realtor. So much for having fun! After several days, we finally found the cutest little two-bedroom home in Winter Garden at 429 Charlotte Street. The price was a whopping $34,500. And believe it or not, we had saved up around $30,000 by then. This was a deal I could not pass up. Why spend $200,000 plus in New York for a home when we could spend this little and live in this beautiful, warm state? It was a no-brainer for me. Our offer was accepted, and we were proud homeowners before we left the state of

Florida. The only thing that was left was to sign the final closing documents about thirty days later. My excitement was great. I could think of nothing else but moving into our first home with my husband and being a homemaker while having a large family, at least four children. I had not yet learned that abusers prefer to have their victims isolated from those who may be able to help them.

We returned to New York and shared the news. We were planning to move sometime that summer after we saved up some more money to furnish the home. This was one of the first major decisions we made, and it was one of the decisions that would allow me, in my later years, to become financially secure.

We closed on the home in April 1989. To my utter surprise, immediately after that, Robbie wanted to move to Florida ahead of me. We had practically no cash, and this was contrary to what we had agreed to. I was unhappy with his decision. How could he leave his wife without feeling any emotion? How could he leave me?

Because we had no money to move yet, Robbie insisted on going so he could start working. I did not want to be separated from him. There were arguments, and of course, I did not want to make waves, so I gave in and he moved to Florida in May 1989, a week or so after we closed on the home. I was supposed to follow soon afterward, sometime in late May or early June.

I was hurt and disappointed that he chose to leave me behind. I was a young, naïve wife who thought there were no other options but to abide by my husband's decisions. Again, I had no concept of alcoholism and how it eventually became his first love and the basis of his decisions. I was never at the top of his priority list. Thinking back, he paid little attention to me or my needs. It was all about what he wanted and nothing else mattered. How did a person as strong as me allow this to happen?

I started to think a lot about my marriage to Robbie once he left for Florida. I repeatedly replayed the incidents in my mind. What had caused him to get so angry to the point where he had to hit someone he was supposed to love? Why the outbursts of severe anger when he did not get his way? And most importantly, why did I give in to him? Was it because I loved him and did not want to see him in this state, or was it because I was scared of what I would do if I had enough strength? I did not have any answers to any of these questions. I was confused.

I was starting to feel detached from Robbie once he left. The first few days were bad. I cried a lot, but as the weeks went on, I felt more and more at ease and less stressed with him gone. At twenty-two, I should not have been stressed! I had no children and no major issues, but when my husband was around I was stressed and hiding from everyone.

We had stopped going to my brother's house to play cards, cook, or eat because Robbie hated going there and despised being around my family. He had started to swear at them in the beginning of our marriage. If he did not want to go, I could not go either. He made sure he created a fuss each time I went by myself. By now, he was swearing a lot, almost all of it directed at my family. I never understood why. He would swear and refer to my brothers, my sisters, and my mom. He never said anything bad about me, but I came from that family, so I wondered how he could claim he loved me but hate everyone I was a part of?

Now I know without a question that this was emotional and verbal abuse. Robbie could not hit me anymore, so he compensated well in other ways. It was also the beginning of the isolation that abusers seek. I did not know it then.

Now that he was in Florida, I could go and enjoy my family. I had really missed them a lot, and I was only a few blocks away. I spent a lot of time with my new nieces and I took them everywhere. Robbie was not around to tell me I could not do what I wanted to do.

I was starting to rethink whether or not the move to Florida was a good one for me. I soon realized it was a really bad idea. I was already starting to get homesick and I hadn't even left yet! How could I leave the only family I knew that loved me? I wasn't sure I wanted to stay with Robbie anymore. My life was happy when he was not around. You see, I had never been apart from my brothers and sisters from the time I was born. As the last of many siblings, I was being taken care of. I was extremely close to my family, and now I was not going to be able to see them on a regular basis. This was not good. This was really not good.

I decided I would not move to Florida, but I did not tell anyone how I felt and what I wanted to do. May came and went, but I did not move. No one asked any questions of me, not even Robbie. Most of them knew Robbie and I were incompatible in many ways, but they supported me; as long as I was happy, they were happy. They did not know I was unhappy because I did not tell them.

May turned to June, and June turned into July. I was still in New York, where I planned to stay. Then the course of my life changed once again.

The company I worked for was closing, and I would be out of a job in a month or so. My boss called me into her office and said she would have to terminate my position with the company. I was a bookkeeper at that time. If she terminated me, I would be able to collect unemployment and I would not have to worry about finding a job right away. I took the offer and changed my mind about staying in New York. I decided to join Robbie in Florida.

Finally, on July 18, 1989, I moved to Florida. My heart was heavy and I felt alone. By then I had started to think about my commitment to the marriage and the oaths I took. I had made this decision to marry the person I loved, and I would have to see it through. I would have to make it work and give it my all. I wish that back then I had been brave enough to talk about my feelings to someone who could have given me some sound advice, but I was full of pride and ego so I kept it all in and never told a soul how sad I was.

When I arrived in Florida, Robbie was happy to see me. We had been apart for almost three months. This was like a lifetime for me. I had grown up a lot in those months. At twenty-two, I had the mind-set of a forty-year-old when it came to finances. I was ambitious, smart, and knew what I wanted. However, I was also emotionally immature to some extent. I had not yet learned that I had the right to change my mind.

There was no doubt in my mind I loved Robbie, and I was still hopeful he would eventually learn to be a good husband. I hoped the anger and drinking would end once he saw how much I loved him. It was a wish and a dream that he would have changed in the three months. I was hopeful that I had the ability to change him. Little did I know that I have the power to change only myself and no one else. I now know I had that power but I failed use it wisely. People must want to change because it is the right thing for them.

The rest of 1989 and 1990 went by quickly. Throughout that time, there was a lot of drinking and many, many endless fights. No matter what

I did or said, Robbie was not listening. He was angry when he did not get his way or when I stood up to him. I got frustrated beyond imagination, so I would go off with my neighbor and friends to be out of the house.

Of course, no one in my family knew since they were in New York. Each time a member of my family came to visit, it caused a series of fights. Robbie would make it clear he did not want them at the house. Of course, when they came, he would treat them well. He would cook, drink, and entertain. Everyone saw only this side of Robbie. I saw both sides. Rarely did anyone see the bad side, his real side. He saved this for me to experience.

Robbie drank daily, and I tried to talk to him about the drinking and how it might cause health problems later. He would not listen. He would respond by either drinking more, breaking plates, or getting in his car and driving away, drunk. I eventually told him I would not tolerate him drinking at home. This caused another set of arguments and huge fights. But Robbie was a resourceful guy. He would stay away from home and drink with friends after work. He would return home drunk very often. My unhappiness was increasing by leaps and bounds.

The year 1990 ended. I decided I would do what I needed to do to get by and stay in the marriage. I came up with the perfect solution. I realized I had no control over Robbie. I had control only over my life. So I decided I would go back to school and build a solid career. At least I had control over that. I was starting to see no end to his abusive behavior and certainly no end to the drinking. But in the end I would have educated myself and gotten into a career that would support me without anyone's help. I was willing, able, and ready to make that sacrifice for myself. I was slowly, very slowly starting a change process and I did not even know it.

I started going to Valencia Community College at nights, four days a week after work in January 1981. I was out of the house and keeping busy. I was away from emotional and verbal abuse. I was basically practicing detachment and did not know it. I learned that this was a safe decision, as I was not around to argue and possibly get into fights.

Robbie was proud and told everyone that I was going back to school. He was happy, and I felt his total support. Now looking back, was it total support for me or total elation at having all that free time to drink? Now I know it was the latter. Sadly, he was elated at my being gone. This was exactly where he wanted to be all along. This truth broke my heart into a million pieces later in my life, a truth I would wish upon no one. The truth that the person I loved possibly never loved me back.

A person who claimed to love me began keeping me away from my family and was unhappy mingling with them. I will be aware in the future that this may be a sign of a strained relationship. I will not close my eyes to the fact that it could lead to other issues, such as abuse.

Nothing Beats Higher Education

Money for liquor, all the time in the world, and no one to answer to: a dream for an active alcoholic.

I really liked school. Being a bookworm most of my life, going back to a formal class setting was food to my soul. I felt right where I needed to be. This was my turf. I would get lost in the library after classes ended around 10:00 p.m. I didn't have to rush home because I knew Robbie wouldn't be home until the drinking stopped around 11:00 p.m. This was working out great for both of us. I was becoming stronger by the day.

I was defining my goals and becoming one focused student. I was OK with ignoring the situation at home in hopes it would go away on its own with no effort from either of us. This is what I named "ostrich syndrome." I simply stuck my head in a hole thinking once in a while that I would pull it out when it was safe. As long as I ignored the sadness, it did not exist. It was too painful to face, so I ignored it. I had not learned yet how to deal with all my emotions in a healthy way. I buried my pain and chose not to deal with it. I pretended I was happy. I told everyone I was happy.

I would get up at 6:00 a.m., fix breakfast and lunch for both of us, go off to work, work all day, and then go to school at night, Monday through Thursday. I would get home, cook, clean the house spotless, and then cook for the next day. Robbie did not know how to cook at this point, so I was starting to teach him since he'd asked. He liked his food a lot, and since I was at school, he had to cook sometimes if he got home before I did. I was busy doing housework, yard work, and homework.

Those who knew my home would see I kept it in mint condition; my yard was full of flowers and well groomed. Robbie did some work and would help in the yard after I would complain. He had a lot more free time and was usually gone a lot. He did a few home improvement projects with a lot of coaxing from me. He rarely did anything voluntarily. If it were entirely up to him, the house would fall apart and the lawn would stay overgrown.

What about all this support I got from him, you ask? Well, the truth shall be told. Robbie never supported my going to school. My workload at home did not change as I started school. Nevertheless, I ensured that our life was polished and looked great to everyone looking in. Robbie worked and would cut the grass and do home improvements after I complained and begged. I was pushing to get things done or threatening to hire someone.

I was making myself happy. I thought that he would eventually change or I had an ability to help him change. I was hopeful and my faith was strong. Hope and faith are two powerful tools to have when in crisis. They literally got me through my years of pain. They helped me get by each day and helped me to stay committed to the person I loved and wanted to be with. Was it low self-esteem on my part? Was I a codependent? Was I an enabler? Was I weak? Was I a victim of abuse? There was a brief moment in time when I used to think so. But as I am writing this book, I am not quite certain nor I am able to ascertain fully the extent of abuse or my behavior and manner of thinking. I believe I avoided facing most of it and internalized my pain and emotions. This was apparently my survival technique. I know I was truly in love and wanted my husband to be happy at the expense of my own happiness. He knew I loved him. There was no question about that. To this day, he could never deny that fact.

In the early years, we would occasionally go fishing and to flea markets, but those times were starting to dwindle away. This was only four years into our marriage. Was this what a marriage was supposed to be like? I think not. After a few months of my going to school and paying close attention to schoolwork and grades, Robbie started to demonstrate more serious anger outbursts. He would get home late and order me to get his dinner, even though it was cooked and on the stove. I started to say no a lot. This did not sit well at all. He would repeatedly slam his plate full of food on the floor or the wall or the sink when he was drunk and upset. A couple of times he grabbed my textbooks and tossed them to the other side of the room. More than once I called the police, and they came out to the house. Robbie told the cops he'd made a mistake and then asked for forgiveness.

A female cop came once, and she asked if Robbie had a drinking problem. I adamantly said no. I honestly believed he did not. Even though his actions proved otherwise, I denied it. What was wrong with me?

I realize that educating myself, especially since I am a victim of an alcoholic abuser, is critical, as it allows me to become financially independent. I am able to provide the necessities for myself and for my children. Without a higher education, I am not sure if I would have been able to break away.

The Grand Entrance

My son, I will love you for all times.

I had already decided I was not having any children. Robbie had said that he did not want any. It was going to be him and me living with each other forever. This, I thought at the time, was the nicest thing anyone had ever said to me. I thought it meant he loved me so much that he did not want to have any children to keep us from each other. My God, what was wrong with me? Was I that stupid and gullible? Yes, I was, sad but true. I fell for that manipulative line and believed not having children was the best decision he ever made for us.

Guess what? I did not remain stupid and gullible for long. The year was 1991. I decided I would have a kid. This was what I wanted. Robbie was my husband, and whether he liked it or not, I wanted a child. I told him I would like to have a child, and then I came off the birth control. I don't really remember if he got angry, but I'm sure he did. I must have blocked it out with the other painful events I forced myself to forget.

I became pregnant in April 1991, exactly three months after stopping the birth control pills. It was a great pregnancy. I was happy, working, going to school, doing homework, doing housework, doing yard work, and anything else my energy allowed. I was on a roll. Robbie was not making any changes. He was drinking more and more.

Christmas 1991 came. I was four weeks from the birth of my firstborn. Robbie and I were always throwing huge house parties, which Robbie loved mainly for the drinking and I loved for the socializing and the company. It also made Robbie happy, and when he was happy, I was happy. I love people and love to give to others. The party was a birthday party for Robbie's cousin's daughter, who was two years old.

I do not remember a lot, but I do remember this. Someone spilled drinks on the floor. We had tiled floors in the great room where the party was. Robbie was drinking a lot and was possibly drunk by then. He came to me and said there was a spill on the floor. Without thinking I got a towel and went over to the area and started to bend down to wipe the floor. I was eight months pregnant. Robbie stood there with a beer in his hand, watching me struggling to bend down. At the time, I did not see anything wrong with that. Robbie never thought for a minute that I was not in any condition to be bending down. I remember thinking about that for a long time. I still think about it today. I felt he truly he did not care. Back then this was unthinkable, so I did the only thing I could do—stuck my head in a hole and hoped in all would go away someday.

My firstborn, Randy, came into this world at 9:00 p.m. on January 23, 1992. He was 6.5 pounds and twenty-one inches long. After six hours of labor pains, he came and went straight into his dad's arms. I was drugged out, feeling good, and tired.

This was one of two major events in my life that would give me peace and happiness. I learned over the years that happiness is to have someone to love and to be loved by them. I now had someone to love that would love me back.

I enjoyed the entire first year of Randy's life. Every time I could, I was with Randy. I took him everywhere. By late 1992, my work travels had started. I would travel throughout the Eastern United States from South Carolina to South Florida. I would also travel to California for training when we would complete acquisitions. Some travels also took to me New Mexico. I regret having to stop breast-feeding before Randy was a year old. I was gone from home often, and I missed Randy a lot. His dad took care of him and never complained about my being gone. He did what needed to be done for his son. Before I left on every trip, I ensured the laundry was done and that the formula and food for Randy was in order. All clothes and bags for the baby-sitter were ready. All Robbie had to do was feed him when he picked Randy up from the sitter and put him to bed. The baby-sitter would bathe Randy before Robbie got him. Life, I believe, was great for Robbie. This would be the freedom he craved to drink and the freedom I craved to be away from the abuse.

I should look out for signs of selfishness in a relationship. I believe a selfish person may not be able to make another truly happy, as they are more concerned with what they can get rather than what they can give.

Thoughts of a Breakup

*Unfortunate are those who continue to
plan but fail to execute the plan.*

The first year of Randy's life went by way too quickly. With work, traveling, school, and a one-year-old, there was no time for anything else. Robbie was continuing to drink a lot, and the arguments were starting to escalate. He would argue over anything. I would sit and pray, hoping that when he came home he would be in a good mood. This was wishful thinking. He was nice when he was with others out drinking, so why couldn't he be nice when he got home? There were few times he was nice. How could he love me and hate everything and everyone around me? Was this possible? I still have no answers.

Yes, back to ostrich syndrome. This was my time out. I loved ignoring the obvious such as the swearing and hatefulness toward those around me. I would go to bed and cry, saying to myself, *It will be better tomorrow.*

Are you thinking I was a little off on reality? Of course, you are. Not really. I wanted the three of us to be happy and was willing to do whatever it took to save this marriage, even if I had to do it alone. I believed that as long as one of us wanted to save it, it would be saved. I now know I was trying to convince myself of the impossible.

The years dragged on. Nothing changed. It was getting worse. I was now twenty-seven years old and had completed my two years at the community college. I had transferred my credits to University of Central Florida toward my four-year degree in accounting. I was finally starting to feel pressured and even starting to break.

At twenty-five years old, I'd felt like ninety. At twenty-seven, I felt like one hundred! I started to develop insomnia and could not sleep at all. This went on for years. I was struggling to keep down my internal turmoil and to maintain that serene, stoic look. I used to be able to do this so easily.

Could five years of marriage do this to a person? Could five years of mental and emotional struggle do this to a perfectly normal and sane person? The answer, like the answers to my other questions, came years later. I learned that alcoholism is a slow and gradual disease, and we adapt to the symptoms without knowing it, little by little.

I was starting to feel trapped and getting close to depression. I knew I had to do something or else I felt I was going to lose my mind. Robbie was continuing to drink a lot. He would pick up Randy from the baby-sitter later and later and drunker and drunker. I knew he was driving Randy while he was drunk.

How did this not bother me? Was this how I demonstrated love for my son, by allowing a drunk driver to endanger his life? I felt like I was going insane! Looking back, I am sure I was not thinking clearly and was possibly going insane. I was becoming a lousy mother and had no concern for myself. I was eating a lot more and started to put on weight. I had been around 125 pounds at five feet six inches. I found myself creeping up toward 130, 135, 140. I was sure at the time I was handling things perfectly fine. Since I did not utter a word to anyone in my family, I did not ask for nor did I receive any help whatsoever. I was not sleeping, and I was on edge and nervous all the time.

An outside observer would probably not see any signs of stress. However, on the inside, I was a total mess. My gut was tight and I felt like throwing up a lot. I would occasionally throw up when arguments would start. I started to get the most horrible headaches. I lost my ability to sleep completely by the time I was twenty-eight years old.

I was starting at the four-year university, and my grades were also slipping from a 3.9 to about a 3.1 GPA. This was not good. I was losing focus despite my best efforts. I was not able to concentrate. I was unable to remember a lot of what I was reading. This was unusual since all my life I had loved school. I aced exams and did not have to study much. Now I found myself spending long hours studying and not remembering much.

Speaking of studying, I tried at all costs not to study when Robbie was home. Somehow I felt he hated it. This, I realized later in life, was a problem. I was focusing on myself, and since he wanted focus on himself, my studying took the focus from him.

One night he came home drunk about 11:00 p.m. I was on the porch sofa studying. I remember clearly it was Business Law II. I had pulled a C in Business Law I, which I'd barely passed. Law was a struggle for me since it's not as black-and-white as accounting. I had to study harder, and Law II was a lot more intense with a lot of writing and opinions on case studies. I had cooked dinner. Robbie walked in and ordered me to get his dinner. I was tired and had had enough. I told him to go get it himself. He grabbed the textbook from my hands and tossed it way across the room, swearing and arguing. He came toward me as if he would hit me.

I was scared. I could barely walk. I was shaking from nervousness and a severe lack of sleep. I called the local Winter Garden Police. The same female officer came to the house who had come before. She asked Robbie a few questions and asked me a few questions. She told me to take a good look at where this was going. She saw me as really wanting to succeed, but my husband was up to no good. She told me he drank too much, and if he continued, I would have issues that would cause severe stress in my life. She told me to think of my son and what impact it would have on him. He was young, she said, and if I left now, he would not remember any of this. She gave me some telephone numbers for places that I could go to for help and to get a good perspective on what I needed to do. I kept the numbers, thinking that this was exactly what I was going to do.

The next day I took off from work and waited for Robbie when he came home from work. I had already decided I was leaving for New York and not coming back. This was a decision I made that night. I told him that as soon as the classes were over, I was going to New York to look for a job and to settle in at my sister's. Robbie did not say much. He was quiet, as usual when confronted sober. I was starting to think he did not care at all about what happened to our marriage and relationship, or even care what happened to our son.

We did not talk for weeks, and exams finally came. I took them, passed the classes, and took time off from my job. I told them I needed to take a long vacation. I took the train with Randy and my neighbor to New York. I still had not told anyone in my family what I was doing. I wish I had started talking to those in my family I trusted the most, like Lakhram.

During the train ride to New York, my mind was racing with fear and confusion. I had made myself a promise to see this marriage it through.

What was I doing? I was going back on a promise I'd made to myself! This was out of character for me. By now, it had been almost a year since I'd developed insomnia. I was now about 155 pounds and approaching size 12. This was from a size 6 a few years ago! I was eating a lot. I did not know until years later this would be my escape from years of pain. It was the summer of 1995, and Randy was around three years old. My marriage was only eight years old, though it felt like a century, close to what I felt in age myself as well.

I stayed at my sister's in New York. I tried to act and look normal, and I thought I did pretty well. No one noticed my internal state of turmoil and pain. I went to meet with Robert Half and Associates, an accounting recruiting firm. I did the normal interview, resume, and put my feelers out. I did not call Robbie or talk to him.

After about a week, Robbie showed up in New York. He came to my sister's house, and we had a fight. I do not remember a lot of it. I knew I was ashamed that my family was there and would finally get to find out my marriage was not a bed of roses and I was failing. This bothered me the most. I never wanted to fail. I wanted to succeed at everything I endeavored to do. I was not going to be labeled a failure, even at the cost of my sanity. I was also sure at the time that if I stayed married and tried harder, he would change. In a sad way, I thought I could really make him better if I did all the right things.

That night after the fight, I fell into the trap of the "make up." Yes, we made up. How many times had I fallen into this trap before? Why was I doing this to myself over and over again? Robbie would argue and swear and argue and swear until I gave in to get him to shut up and go to sleep. I started to hate intimacy more and more. I used to love it. It was one of the most calming experiences of my life to be truly intimate with someone I loved. I would realize later that I did not really hate it; I hated whom I was having intimacy with! Years of abuse have some crucial consequences.

Finally, I decided to go back to Florida with Robbie. We took the eighteen-hour trip with Robbie driving all the way back home. I was throwing up the whole trip, sick to my stomach about how I'd given in. I knew it was the wrong decision, but what prompted me to give in? I realized now a Higher Power was in control. He was about to give me another gift.

I should not have left issues after issues unresolved. Soon they built up and became unmanageable. I should have taken some action and started resolving them. I now know problems do not just go away. Someone has to start working on them, and that may be me.

My Miracle Child

My daughter, I will love you for all times.

The summer was great. Since I thought I was leaving for New York, I did not enroll in school. This was the first summer since 1991 that I was off. I really enjoyed my time at home with Randy. Robbie was well behaved that summer as well, and I finally said to myself, *He has truly changed.* What a miracle. He was turning out to be the good husband I'd prayed for all those years. This was great.

Little did I know at the time that lifelong behaviors rarely change. I learned later that abusers and alcoholics briefly change when confronted; they may revert to old behaviors when the dust settles.

I started to give away Randy's old baby stuff to my neighbor, who was pregnant. Robbie and I did not plan to have any other children. In my heart, I really wanted more children, but I knew Robbie did not want any more. I was saddened on the inside, but hey, I got Robbie and Randy. That was a great compromise.

A couple of months went by, and it was starting to cool down in Florida. I believe I started to feel bad during a weekend in September 1995. Robbie had left early to help a friend fix some rotted wood on a second-story back deck. He was gone early. I started to feel like I was going to pass out and started throwing up nonstop.

I ran to my car, drove as fast as I could to the drugstore, made a purchase, and came back home. The purchase was a pregnancy test. It was positive! My heart was racing. I thought I was going to pass out. I was so happy; I could only think about telling Robbie. I loaded Randy into the car and shot off to tell him the wonderful news.

I pulled into the friend's driveway and ran up the stairs with Randy in toe. Robbie was standing on the second-story rail doing repairs overhead. All I remember was saying,

"Guess what? I'm pregnant!"

He almost fell off the railing. My goodness, I think I ruined his whole day and possibly the rest of his life! Only then did I remember he did not want another kid. He said nothing. I was crushed. I felt pain at his coldness and lack of care and concern. But who cared? I could do this all by myself, and he would eventually learn to accept it and love the baby.

I was sick the entire pregnancy. At around six months, I had put on a lot of weight. My left hip had dislocated, and I was having a hard time walking and sleeping. Insomnia was still a factor. I was also eating a lot.

At around seven months I had to sleep in a recliner to prevent breathing issues. Thank God for the great bosses I had. I was able to work from home a lot toward the latter part of my pregnancy. I was in school the entire time, my belly touching my desk. I intended to stay in school. This was something I was sure I needed to put us in a financially secure position. This sacrifice was for my family.

It's funny how things change in our lives as time goes on. I was starting to feel happier. At least, I thought I was. I do not remember a lot at this particular point in my life. I wonder why. I remember being overweight toward the last couple of months, but I do not remember much during the pregnancy.

At the peak of my pregnancy, I was a whopping 190 pounds. Sam entered the world around 8:00 p.m. on April 18, 1996, following an induced labor and thirteen agonizing hours of pain. She was 8.6 pounds and one fat baby girl. She completed my life. I now had a son and a daughter. Nothing could go wrong; we were now the perfect married couple and perfect family.

Again, Robbie held her first and fell in love with her instantly. Like Randy, she tugged at his heart. He was proud of her, and I knew he would love her forever. I knew he would also spoil her. That was fine with me. We had suffered in the early years of Randy's life, but we could make up for that. Those were my thoughts at the time, thoughts mainly to comfort me.

I now know people seldom share my enthusiasm for a number of reasons. I believe if I am passionate about something then I will go ahead and achieve it, sometimes to the detriment of relationships. I will not let anyone steal my convictions or erode my passion for my cause.

A New Beginning

We attract what we feel.

That first year of Sam's life was a happy one for all of us. Robbie made tremendous improvements in his life. He stopped smoking on December 31, 1996. He also eased up drinking and going out drinking. He did a great job with both children. This allowed me to work, to go to school, and to advance my career. It seemed we were great together. Robbie still did not complain when I would go off for work-related travel.

During the summer months, I would take Randy and Sam off on vacations, mostly to the beach. We never traveled with Robbie. Randy and Sam loved getting on a plane and traveling. I was not pushing Robbie to join us. He would have to make that choice for himself. He made a choice, but not to come with us.

There were times when I would cry myself to sleep thinking of how much of my happiness I was giving up to remain married. I bottled up my stress inside me, and I released it only when I was alone in the form of crying. I hated being alone, so I kept myself busy. I was extremely lonely and sad on the inside. That forced me to think about myself, which made me more horribly sad and depressed.

I was starting to think about how we could grow our assets to secure the future of our children. I was saving a lot of money. By now, I was starting to make about forty thousand dollars annually. This was a lot of money since we had no mortgage. Robbie was making about twenty-five thousand dollars a year. He was not working on a regular basis. He took care of the children, worked around the home, and cooked. I was really starting to sink into accepting the marriage for what it was, forgetting the past or burying it, one or the other. We did not argue or fight a lot during the first few years of Sam's life.

I was about to complete my studies in accounting at UCF and had a few classes left before I graduated. My salary was starting to match my level of education, and I started to realize going to school was one of the wisest decisions I had made in my life. I would later learn that without the education, I would have suffered a lot in the later years of my life.

The year was 1997, and I was starting to look for another piece of real estate on which to build a home. I had grown up in the most rural parts of Guyana. I love the outdoors and love to garden, and I wanted to relive those years. From there, I would live, love, raise the children, be a family, and retire with Robbie. In my mind, life would be perfect as I knew it then.

I started the search for a piece of paradise. I wanted to be around water and an open space. I found ten acres in Howey in the Hills. It had a lot of open space and a nice pond that wrapped around half the property. I made an offer and it was accepted. I had not told Robbie of the offer or acceptance, as it would have resulted in a fight or constant nagging and arguing. It was late 1997, and the seller did not want to close that year due to an excess in capital gains tax. He asked if I could wait until 1998 to close on the sale. This gave me many months before I had to tell Robbie about the purchase and ask for his signature on the purchase agreement.

Finally, the year ended and it was time to tell Robbie he was the proud owner of ten acres of land. Who was going to do that? Not me! So, I engaged the help of my loyal realtor friend. We arranged for Robbie to take a ride out to see a property we "might" like, not telling him I'd already bought it and all I needed was his signature of approval. I am not proud of this decision and I hated making it behind Robbie's back.

As we pulled in, the lake water was high to the edge of the pond, and there were fish and lily pads with blooming white flowers. It was apparently stocked with fish, as you could see them frolic and play from the edge of the pond. I forgot about Robbie and how upset he would be once he found out I had already made the purchase. Once he saw the lake and the fish, he was hooked. He loved fishing, and I was sure he'd started dreaming of the days he could be out here fishing and relaxing with his son. The timing was perfect. The setting was great. Robbie was willing signed the papers. He looked at me and smiled. I really don't remember much after that. The deal was closed, and we became proud landowners of two parcels of prime real estate.

I immediately started talking about going there to live, but each time the discussion came up, Robbie would get really, really angry. He said it was a long way to come to work each day—yet he drove out there each day on his own. On weekends, he would go more than once a day. What was going on? Why did he not want to move there if he was going there every day? This was mind blowing. I did not understand it then or even now. I ignored the opposition and went ahead with looking for a house plan and prices. Like everything else, I knew once we settled in, Robbie would be fine. He would see the wisdom in my decisions and would forget about all the anger he was feeling. I felt I had the power to change him and assured myself I could fix anything, even another person's shortcomings.

I realized we did not have enough money to have the home built by a contractor. We did not even have enough money to get an architect to do the drawing. That would cost thousands of dollars. I started to think outside the box and sought other ways to cut costs. I found a company that sold pencil drawings of house plans for under five hundred dollars that could be modified to fit any state. I purchased a set of rough sketches and started to modify them to fit Florida's requirements. It took me about a month, and when I felt I'd come close, I took it to an engineer to approve, sign, and seal. The whole process cost under $1,200. We saved over $10,000 in that process.

In the meantime, school had ended. I had one class left and could not take it until winter of 1999. It was great to have the time off between the summer of 1998 and January 1999. This allowed me to complete the house plans and look at the option of owner/builder. I obtained the permit to build the home. In addition, we were able to hire a general contractor to oversee the work. We had no choice but to subcontract the work out ourselves. It cost too much to have a builder build it.

I opened an equity line on our home in Winter Garden since there was no mortgage against it. I was really trying to get Robbie involved in the process. Despite his protests to me, he told everyone about the property and how we were going to build our own home there soon. Yet when I attempted to have a discussion with him about the home, he would begin an argument about how he would never move there and that he was OK with use getting a divorce. This was extremely confusing for me.

Around the same time, Robbie was beginning to drink a lot again. I complained and he found ways to hide it. Not one time when I asked if he drank did he answer yes. He could be falling over, but no, he did not drink. I did not even bother to argue or tell him how I felt anymore.

In September 1998, we started building our home in Howey in the Hills. The process was not as painful as I had initially thought. We had a bank that did the construction loan, and we managed the subcontractors and worked with the City of Tavares on each stage to ensure the contractors were performing up to city codes. On Christmas Eve 1998, the shell of the home was completed. The rest of the work was up to us.

Robbie became extremely involved in the building of the home from that point on. He would spend all his time at the home working by himself for long, long hours and late into the night. I saw little of Robbie during the time he was working on the house, but I was proud of him. I knew he would eventually come around to appreciating it all. We painted on Christmas Day and a few days after that. Little by little the walls, cabinets, flooring, windows, and trim were finished. In March of 1999, the City of Tavares did their final walk-through and issued the Certificate of Occupancy for us to move in. We moved into our brand-new home in early spring of 1999.

I believe that in a healthy relationship there is no need to hide or mask the truth. If I see this happening, I will try to find out why it is happening to me and address it appropriately. I learned that lying leads to more lying. The truth is easier to remember. I don't have to keep track of it.

Early Years in Howey in the Hills

Change does not come easily, especially without effort.

We rented our Winter Garden home to my sister, Devika. This was another reason for Robbie to drink, swear, and complain. He called my sister every bad word he knew from *bitch* to *whore* and any other degrading word he could think of. He would go to Winter Garden every day to see the house and, of course, made a lot of pit stops along the way to drink. By the time he made it home, he was drunk and ready for a fight. I never knew anyone else who could argue as much as Robbie.

The first year in our new home was one of the most miserable years we spent together. The verbal and emotional abuse was at an all-time high. It was a daily routine I was definitely not handling it well or as well as I used to in the past. We'd had some good years, from when Sam was born up until April 1999. I was approaching my midthirties and Robbie was about forty years old. I was starting to feel I could not contain my moods and internalize them as I had in past years. What was happening to me? I was not able to handle this madness anymore! I was praying to God for help. I was confused a lot. I also started to drink more and more to forget how I was feeling or to fall asleep and not have to listen to Robbie's constant nagging. The numbness of the alcohol worked temporary wonders for me.

Sometime in 2000 I invited Robbie's mother to visit us. I talked to her about Robbie's behavior and continued excessive drinking, arguing, and swearing. I also told her I was not sure if I was going to be able to handle his behavior. Robbie complained how he was in the new home "all alone" and had no friends. He was in Orlando every day, drinking, and yet he complained. I was starting to think he wanted out of the marriage. He would constantly tell me he wanted to get out of this "shit" he was in. I was at a loss as to what was contributing to his behavior and what "shit" he was referring to. How could someone who was never home complain about being home too much?

His mother was as confused as I. She was not able to get an answer from Robbie as to the cause of his behavior. She asked him many questions, but Robbie remained quiet and would not respond. She must have felt what I felt—all those years of not understanding what happened or went wrong. Sadly, Robbie's mother left after about a week, and I was again left alone to deal with my issues.

What did I do about it? Yes, ostrich syndrome came back. It was my escape. I had earned my bachelor's degree in accounting. In 1999, I'd purposely gone off to school to avoid all this abuse and alcohol, and it seemed I would have to do the same again. The pain was too much to sit around and endure. So I ran off to graduate school and took on more work that caused me to be out of town a lot. I started my MBA in 2000 while studying to take the Certified Public Accountant (CPA) exam. I had no time to stop.

Again, insomnia was starting to come back after a brief pause. I could not sleep. I was putting weight back on after working really hard to get back to a size 8. I was bent on passing the CPA exam the first time. I took the Becker review course, I took graduate classes, I traveled for work, and I tended to our children and home as best as I could manage; but I was going into a serious depressive state. My mind could not relax. There were times I thought I was going to have a nervous breakdown. Everything was starting to get to me, even the kids.

The one time I felt everything was a little manageable was when I was out of the home. Being home for me meant being around a person who was on edge, always swearing, always yelling at Randy and Sam, smashing plates, and tossing anything he could get his hand on. Drinking contributed greatly to the behaviors. When Robbie was not drunk, he would purposely start an argument to allow him to leave and drink. The cycle continued over many years.

I started to pull away from him. I stopped going to parties and other functions. I had been Robbie's designated driver, enabling him to drink when we went out. Once I stopped, I felt I was of no use to him. He saw me as a person who brought in the money, kept the house spotless, and took care of the children. I felt my whole world falling apart, and all I was doing was standing by and watching it unfold and crumble away. I was afraid to take a stand since that meant causing more arguments. I could not handle any more arguments. I took my children away from home as much as I could. We would go off to the movies until midnight or to the mall, just anywhere but home. I was running from my own home! My paradise had turned in a virtual place of pain and suffering.

Before all this, I would have a few glasses of wine a week. Now I found I was drinking half a bottle or more each evening. This was my escape when I was at home. The years flew by. They were miserable, but they flew. I ended up passing the CPA exam and obtained my master's degree. I became a licensed CPA in the state of Florida in 2003. Becoming a CPA was not my goal; running away from home was. I ran and ran straight into being a CPA!

By now, my salary was pushing one hundred thousand dollars annually. Robbie continued to drink. If I complained long enough, he would curtail his behavior for a few months, but never more than two or three months at a time. Then, he would revert to the old habits as soon as the dust settled. Was this going to be how the rest of my life would be? I was now 176 pounds and approaching a size 16! I was overweight and felt I was about to have a nervous breakdown. I was eating constantly. I hated myself. I hated what I had become.

Despite all this, when I thought of the marriage ending, I shivered. I could not imagine my life without Robbie in it or even entertain thoughts of a divorce. I truly loved him and truly wanted to be married forever. I didn't think I was weak or had low self-esteem; nor was I insecure. I was none of those things. I truly loved him. Those were my thoughts at the time. The reality of walking away was literally crippling. I could not do it. I would stick it out, even if it cost me my life. There was no way out for me. No way. I was fearful of the emotional pain it would cause me, my children, and Robbie. So I stayed and coped the best way I knew how: avoidance and denial.

Falling in love does not mean ignoring my feelings. I should be able to love another as well as focusing on how I am feeling. However, I believe we should make compromises for those we love. Someone who truly loves me will not expect compromises, but will be pleasantly surprised by them.

The Longest Ending

*Running to escape my problems is not
the way to deal with them.*

I was completely done with school. There was no higher I could go in my field of study unless I wanted a doctoral degree costing over fifty thousand dollars. No, that would not happen. How long would I run from my pain? I'd learned the hard way that running did nothing. It only buried the pain deeper and deeper and delayed the inevitable. It did nothing to the pain except to grow it and nurture it. The pain went with me everywhere I went.

I was really starting to drink a lot by now. I hated traveling and no longer wanted to leave home. I wanted to be at peace and to be happy. I was not even thinking about Randy and Sam anymore. I had completely forgotten about them by 2004. I was having lots of aches and pains throughout my body, from my knees to my back and shoulders. I had to go to the hospital after collapsing at home with kidney stones. My right knee was sore. I was only thirty-eight years old, and God, I was falling apart, one body part at a time! Something had to change or else I was sure I would be dead before I was forty! I had given up riding my bicycle or engaging in other forms of exercise. I looked ill and felt worse.

Each time I went to the doctor, he would prescribe pain medications such as hydroquinone, Percocet, or muscle relaxers. I was told not to drink while on those medications, but I was finding it hard not to drink. I could not handle the daily arguments and abuse unless I had had a few drinks. So, I drank and took the pain pills. It felt good, probably euphoric. I was able to zone out in a flash and ignore everyone, including my beautiful children.

I had discovered a new way of managing my marriage since traveling for work was now minimal. Drinking alcohol and taking prescription drugs worked out well for me. Everyone was a burden to me. The children were obstacles in my way. They were always around, and I had to hide to take my drugs of choice. I was constantly yelling at them. I ignored Robbie, the object of my initial frustration. I tried to read a lot and listen to music through headphones. With no luck focusing on either, I would not cook or clean and would leave the dishes in the sink. All I could do was work, come home, get my fix, and ensure the children did their homework and ate well. I slept a lot. I did not want anyone to speak to me. We went nowhere, no movies and no malls like we used to visit on Fridays or Saturdays. I made only necessary trips to the grocery store.

I hated when friends or family called to come over. I made every excuse I could think of to avoid them. This was an invasion of my privacy and my insanely perfect life. I stopped talking to my family as much. Sadly, I became a scary echo of Robbie's behavior.

One of my brothers, his wife, and their youngest child were visiting the summer of 2004. I hated it. It meant I would have to listen to constant bickering and complaining. Robbie fought with me the entire time they were with us. He treated my family as if they had a life-threatening, contagious disease that he did not want to contract. I allowed him to treat my family like crap. I did not want to create a conflict because if I did, they would know we were not the perfect family. I had to hide this deep so no one would know. I had to look happy, and boy, it was getting harder and harder to do that. I had to drink more and take more pills to get through the day. Work was the only escape I had, so I worked as much as I could.

When my family wasn't visiting, fights were limited since I was not talking and getting upset anymore. I was usually in my own imaginary world of make-believe. I would zone out from Robbie. I was overweight and not doing anything to lose weight, nor did I even want to. I did not care anymore. I simply gave up. Yes, I, the fighter, finally gave up. Hard to believe it myself, but it was true. I was starting to think a lot about giving up my life as well. What would happen if I died? That would be great! The pain would go away. I wouldn't feel it anymore. Wow, that was the ultimate solution. If I chose to live, I would get fatter, drink, and take prescription pills, and eventually the end would come. So, I would have to make the end come sooner. I was no procrastinator. I planned well to speed up a process. Why wait to die slowly and in pain? I could change that. These were the thoughts of a depressed person possibly on the verge of a nervous breakdown.

I learned I should not put my trust and faith in alcohol to help solve my problems. In addition, I believe a person who is impaired by alcohol tries to complicate issues, which I think is deflection. I know it is difficult to remove oneself from an environment that involves an addiction. Habits form slowly and discreetly but are difficult to break.

An Animal's Instinct

If animals could speak, I wonder what stories they will tell

It was Saturday, August 21, 2004. My brother and his family were visiting, along with Devika. The night before my brother had been practically begging Robbie to take him fishing. Robbie kept on making up every excuse not to take him. I felt sad for my brother and helpless in the situation. I had lost my fight to live at this point. I had finally lost myself.

At dinner that night, Robbie started an argument over who was sitting in his spot on the sofa! I was shaking and wanted to throw up. I had tried so hard to hide this, but now it was starting to come out. What would my family think? I was so focused on what everyone thought that I forgot about myself. I never thought about my feelings or health or what I was doing to my body. What was happening to me? Was I losing my mind? I had finally crossed the line between sanity and insanity. I could not think rationally any longer.

The next morning we were having breakfast when Robbie came rushing in through the back door of the house. He was breathless. It was around 9:00 a.m. He stormed into the garage and took out the shotgun. I was in total shock and so was the rest of my family. What was going on? Robbie tried to go outside again but collapsed on the living room sofa. The two-thousand-pound bull he had been raising on our land since birth had attacked him. Robbie was gored in the right chest under the breast area. This was a gentle, yet majestic animal that attacked its only known keeper, a keeper who had fed him by hand when he was a few days old.

It was a deep puncture, and I could clearly see white tissue from the wound on his chest. My head was in total confusion. Robbie was going to die—I knew it! I did not want this. I wanted to die, not him. I had to save him. The love I felt for him was enormous at that moment. I did not want to lose him.

We got in the car and drove to the nearest express care in Leesburg. The doctor took Robbie's vitals and said he would die in an hour if he did not get trauma treatment immediately, but she refused to treat him. Instead, she called an ambulance to transport him to the nearest hospital; the paramedics came and refused to take him as well. He was passing out quickly. I overheard one of the paramedics say, "He won't make it by ambulance. He needs to be airlifted immediately; call Medevac now."

Within minutes there was a Medevac helicopter parked on Highway 441 in the center of the roadway in Leesburg. My brother was with me. I was not functioning well. I thought I was going to faint. I felt weak. I felt pain I had never felt before. I thought I'd felt it all before then, but no. This was pain I had never felt before. This was different, very different. This was a definite change in my life. I was watching the death of the one person I loved, and there was nothing I could do.

This was an event I would never forget. I did not know it at the time, but it was the lowest point in my emotional state. I knew then I could not go any lower. I was sinking fast. My marriage was a mess; I avoided everyone in my life, including my children; and I felt I was worthless. I had never felt worthless in my life, but I had no confidence in any decisions I made. To top it all off, I looked like crap. How could I let myself go like this? I had been a happy person full of life, making jokes, making others feel worthy and important. I led a team of professionals in accounting and finance for a large public company. I managed my work and associates with utmost precision. I made business decisions that were successful in all aspects of the business. Yet I could not make decisions to fix my own personal life and marriage! This was baffling to me. How had I gotten here? What had happened to me? Where had I gone? I had to try to find me. I missed me.

Robbie was flown to Orlando Regional Medical Center and admitted to the trauma center. He was bleeding internally, and the wound had come a quarter inch from piercing the bottom of his heart. He would have been dead on the spot had the horn gone any farther into his chest. He remained in the trauma center for two days before being stabilized. They were about to move him to a regular room, but Robbie insisted on discharging himself. I did not put up a fight over his decision even though he could not even get out of the bed. I had sat with him for forty-eight hours straight.

When he came home, his mother came to stay and I took time off from work. Between the two of us, we tended to all his needs for weeks. We had to help him do everything. I was thinking a lot those days about my life and how I'd let it slip away without a fight.

Robbie was given morphine and Percocet for pain. He was on the medications for a while and was out of work for months. Finally, the prescriptions ran out and he went nuts! He wanted more pills to take the pain away. By now, I was sure the pain was gone or not as intense. I was starting to understand why he needed the drugs. You see, I took prescription drugs myself and knew they were addictive and hard to stop. I was thinking a lot about myself and what this marriage was doing to me. I thought about how much I had been drinking now for about eighteen months. I thought about the countless times I went to the doctor faking my pain to have the prescriptions refilled. As the days went by, I started to see my children again. I mean, really looked them in the eyes. I missed them terribly. I realized I had become a terrible mom. It saddens me to this day.

I decided then to take total responsibility for my actions and what I had done in the past year and a half to myself and to my children. I cried for me. I love both of them so much. How could I do this to the people I love? Worse yet, how could I do this to myself? Was this how I planned to live my life, by running from my problems? No, this was not going to happen to me. One person might not care about this family, but that wouldn't be me. I wanted to live, to love, and to be happy again. No one would stand in my way. No one, Robbie included, would rob me of my life.

I decided to see his injury and recovery to the end and support him in whatever career he chose, but I would put my life back together, one piece at a time. This I was sure of. How did I plan to do it, you ask. I had no clue at the time, but I knew myself and I knew how strong I used to be. I was determined to get back to being me again. I also knew that what lies between people and what they want is the willpower to do it and the faith in themselves. Those two things I had. I was willing, able, and had total faith in my Higher Power. I would save myself and then save my children. This I knew I had the energy to do. I would do whatever it took.

Looking back now, I know what finally opened my mind's eye. A person I loved was dying. I was looking death in the eye, and I knew this life had more to it than dying. I did not want to miss out anymore. I was now about thirty-nine years old. I had many beautiful years ahead of me. I could choose to enjoy them or choose to waste them. I chose to enjoy them. I knew this would affect Robbie. I knew I would have to detach myself from him whichever way possible in order to be able to pick up the pieces of my life. I knew I could face a lot more anger from him and possibly more emotional or physical confrontations. I was ready to face whatever I needed to in order to save my life. So what if I died in the process of trying to save my life? My Higher Power would know I had tried and had not given up. Giving up would mean I did not value the life He gave me when he thought I was worthy of that life.

With birth comes death, but what I do in the journey I call life is entirely up to me. This journey is the path between birth and death. One way or the other I was going to die. I chose to die happy, certainly not in the misery I was in. If I made no change, I would never know what different results could come. It was time I got *me* back into my life.

I believe that in the "garden" we call our life, we are obligated to make ourselves useful, productive, and respectful to every being. If we do not, then we are simply of no use to the garden and stand a chance of becoming an annoying weed, soon to be plucked out and cast aside.

A New Career

Lie once, and many more lies may be needed.

The year 2005 finally came around, and Robbie's injury had healed well. I made a resolution to myself to make a change to get myself well first. I could not help anyone if I was not well. First, I had to stop drinking completely. I had to handle issues with Robbie and then take a stand against him. I was not a weak person, and this was a fight for my life; I would fight to the end. I wanted to walk the rest of my life in peace and happiness with one child on each arm. This was my goal.

It was February and I took some time off with Randy and Sam to go to South Florida. I left them both with a relative and went to the beach for a long walk to plan what I was going to do next. It was cold in Florida at that time. I recall the wind beating down on my face. I was cold as I sat on the beach. I was there for a long time. It was then I decided I needed to write about my feelings to get those feelings out of me and get me into a safe place. Since I still planned not to tell anyone what was really going on, I had to find an outlet. I decided I would write about the events of my horrific situation. I started writing everything that had happened to me from the time I was born, as best as I could recall. That was where this book started. It was meant only to keep my secrets, the ones I did not want anyone to know about. From this point forward, I was able to find my way back from my darkest days. Writing saved my life.

Robbie decided on a new career, driving and delivering merchandise for Federal Express as a subcontractor. He would deliver to post offices in various areas in Florida. I supported him fully. I registered his company and helped in the purchase of his first delivery vehicle. I set up a home office and assisted him in his decisions. I was bent on making him successful and putting my life back together, one day at a time. I was starting to feel stronger and stronger. At first, it was hard not to drink, but I was determined. I started walking and watched what I ate. By the summer of 2005, I had lost fifteen pounds. I was in a size 12 and at about 165 pounds. At least the scale was going backward. This was a good sign. I started to read more and listen to my music again. I was able to focus a little and started to feel moments of happiness. I was bent on ignoring Robbie when he started an argument.

Robbie was working nights from 1:00 a.m. until 10:00 a.m. six days a week. He seemed happy all the time, as he was gone a lot and rarely argued much. He was finally making decent money. This, I found out later, was something he prided himself on. He was not sleeping much at all, though, and this concerned me. I would talk to him about it, and he would fly off the handle, yelling and swearing, accusing me of not wanting him to succeed. His behaviors from before the bull attack were starting to set it again. This time, I would not let them get to me. I was recovering, and no one would stand in the way, including him.

I was also starting to pray a lot more on a regular basis. I put together my prayer altar in the foyer and prayed each morning and each evening, asking my Higher Power to help me find myself. I begged Him to get me out of my pain and promised that if He did, I would ask for nothing except peace and happiness for the rest of my life. I was starting to have hope again. I had lost that hope, and I needed to find it again, one prayer at a time.

Early one morning September 2005, I received a call from a friend of Robbie's saying that Robbie had an accident in Tampa. It was around 5:00 a.m. I left the children asleep and drove as fast as I could to the Tampa area to meet up with Robbie at the side of I-75 in Hillsborough County. His truck was smashed in the rear, and almost all his cargo had been pushed forward. Most packages were damaged. Robbie had been rear-ended by an eighteen-wheeler. Robbie said he was in the right lane driving and saw the truck behind him coming up at a faster pace. Robbie said he held on because he knew the guy was driving way too fast. It was a high-speed impact. The other driver was cut badly in the face from the shattered windshield, and the front of his vehicle was severely damaged.

Robbie said he was not feeling well, so I took him to the emergency room at Tampa Regional Medical Center. They checked him out and gave him painkillers and muscle relaxant. Yes, just what he needed. More painkillers! I also learned that the Highway Patrol had ticketed Robbie for illegally pulling off and on to a highway. The reports said he'd pulled out in front of the other truck. Robbie said the police were lying and that he had been driving in the right lane and never pulled off or on to the highway. He told me the cop was lying. I believed him.

We went to court since we were contesting the charges. The other company sued us. It would take two years to settle the matter, and countless depositions and mediations. Fortunately, the insurance covered most of the cost. However, Robbie was not prepared for the financial setback. He was not able to work for a while. Expenses were piling up along with legal fees. I was OK with him out of work for a while, but this was not good for him. He was home a lot, and I was home a lot. I had lost a lot of weight and was sleeping better. Exercising really helped me relax and kept my focus, and I was writing in my computer journal almost every day. I would write what I would do and how I would do it, putting down my plan to find myself, one word at a time.

Robbie no longer slept much. He was always agitated, and each day it was getting worse. I finally decided I would tell him how I felt and that I would no longer let his behavior impact the children or me. I told him that I did not want him drinking and coming home anymore. I made it clear to him that if he chose to drink, he was to stay wherever he was and come home only when he was not going to argue or cause a fight. I made sure he knew that if I ever caught him drinking and driving with our children, I would call the cops and report him. I had no problem with him losing his license. I was not angry; I simply was tired of all the years of abuse, and I could not allow it to impact my children any longer.

Both kids were quiet growing up. I am sure now they were afraid to talk around the house for fear of repercussions. I may never know how they felt. I wish I'd had had the strength and courage back then to find out how they felt. I missed that opportunity and it saddens me today.

Sadly, I remember little of Robbie's reaction to my changes during this time. I vaguely remember him continuing to swear and being angry, breaking plates, and being gone all the time. I strongly believe my mind blocked this out of my memory permanently. It was probably too painful to remember. As I was writing this book, I was amazed by what I wrote down. If I had not written things down, I truly believe I would have never remembered. I had blocked out so much from my mind. I had to block my pain in order to live and survive each day.

I made a personal commitment not to drink and drive. If I planned to drink, I would first look for a designated driver who would not drink. I know drinking and driving can quickly cause a loss in life, resources, and much pain and regret to a wide range of innocent people.

Personality Changes

*Change is a gradual process that
slowly ascends over time.*

Robbie spent no time with our children by the time 2006 rolled around. He had stopped taking Randy fishing or anywhere else, even to the grocery store. He would not talk to us. When he conversed with Randy and Sam, it took the form of yelling. The only time we saw him was when he came in to eat dinner around 10:00 p.m. each night while we were watching TV. If we so much as looked at him, he would start a fight or toss his plate either in the sink or on the kitchen floor.

I tried to keep quiet and kept both children quiet as well. No matter what we said or did, it caused a fight. Robbie was gone from home almost all the time when I was not there. When he did come home, he avoided me, spending this time either outside when I was inside or inside when I was outside.

I suggested to him maybe his job was stressing him out, but he insisted on working nights and did anything to make that happen. He had replaced his damaged delivery truck and continued with the same job. He would not sleep more than one or two hours straight and got up at least five times during the night to repeatedly check that the door was locked. He checked the doors at least ten times at night and would constantly go outside.

His facial features started to change. He developed dark circles under his eyes, his color started to darken, and he was rapidly losing weight. His cholesterol and blood pressure were not stabilizing, even though he was on medications. He told me his eyesight was going, and he seemed to have a glazed look all the time. He was diagnosed as borderline diabetic at one of his regular six-month checkups. I could not even ask him about his tests; he would explode in a rage and tell me it was none of my business.

There were a lot of inconsistencies with his behaviors. I never knew if he would be quiet, loud, threatening, or argumentative. He could easily switch within seconds from good to bad behaviors. I no longer felt safe anymore around him.

I had lost most of the weight I had put on over the years, and I was more patient with my children and beginning to think clearer. I no longer drank or took any pills, not even a Tylenol. I was feeling much better and no longer felt like I was losing my mind. I wrote down everything I was feeling in my daily writings. It helped me move forward, one day at a time. I thought of the future a lot and what that future held for me.

Eventually Robbie stopped talking to me completely sometime in 2006. I made a promise to myself. I would give it another year and see what happened. I was ready for the long haul. The marriage would not end without some effort on my part. I was willing to keep my mouth shut and be there if and when Robbie needed me. I wanted to be strong for him and our children. I decided I would join a gym and continue to work on myself, and then take better care of Randy and Sam. I was starting to mend the maternal bond with my children. We were going out again to the movies and restaurants. Our family was divided; the children and me with Robbie by himself. But he had chosen this path. There was nothing I felt I could do to bring him back. He was beyond my help. I felt helpless and was sad to see him miserable all the time.

Nothing had changed by the summer of 2006. Robbie continued to lose weight. His explosions of anger and hate became more threatening to himself. He told me on several occasions that he would take his own life and that he wanted to leave our home. He would burst out, saying he wanted to leave and that I should call the cops or else he was going to take his own life. He made it clear he wanted to get out of the house and live his life alone. He claimed he had no problem living alone for the rest of his life. He told me he wanted to go back to Guyana, saying the children were old enough and they no longer needed him. He said I could take everything and give him ten thousand dollars to leave. This was accompanied by his uncontrolled crying.

By this time, I was starting to think the marriage would fail. I could no longer fix it by myself. Again, I came up with the ultimate solution.

I would end my life. I believed this was, at the time, a sane thought. I was not confused, nor was I under any other stress that I could not manage. Remember, it was almost a year into what I called my "recovery." This was something I decided on my own. It would be the solution to all our problems. It would ensure the marriage did not fail. Robbie would have to step up, take responsibility, and change his ways. I would be gone and out of the picture, as I strongly believed I was the source of all his issues. I fully blamed myself for his issues when I made this decision.

Here was my grand plan. I drove the Florida Turnpike each morning to and from work. I always saw vehicles being pulled up from the 561 overpass where they had flipped over. That was the spot where I would drive my car over the rails. I was certain I would die, and everything would be solved in a flash.

That morning I got dressed. It was late spring 2006. I had it all planned in my head. I was a mile from the spot and held on to the steering wheel as tightly as I could. I was now half a mile away, and suddenly I realized I was driving a car that was wrapped in steel and airbags! I would not die. I could not afford to be maimed or injured. I had to be sure I was going to die. I passed the spot. That point in my sane life, I realized I had cross the line from 'sanity to insanity.' This was another turning point. I strongly believe to this day that divine intervention prevented me from going through with my plan. I felt my Higher Powers had other plans for me.

As I passed the spot, I started to cry and I thought about being the mother of my children. Ironically, I never thought about my children no longer having a mom. I never thought about anything other than doing what I needed to do to ensure Robbie changed his ways and the marriage did not end. The thought of ending my marriage was not an option that came close to a realistic consideration. My reality at that time was ending my existence and robbing my children of their mother. I guess when you grow up in a culture where ending a marriage is a difficult option, it is complex even to consider such a thing. I thought about my stupid decision that day at work and came home with a lot in my head. I was happy to see my Randy and Sam that day. I had been sure when I left home that morning that it was the last I was going to ever see my beautiful children.

As a parent, I have a huge responsibility toward my children. Most importantly, I have an obligation to live my life in such a way that my children can emulate me as they formulate their lives.

Taking Charge of My Life

*Bad choices are sometimes easy to make;
consequences, difficult to remove.*

I had joined the Curves for Women gym in the beginning of summer 2006. I went three to five times a week, and one of the trainers tracked my results. I was starting to work more around the home and spend a lot more time with the children. After a few months, around early summer of 2006, I saw visual results of my hard work. I had lost about fifteen more pounds and about eleven inches around various part of my body. I was a lot more energized and was able to avoid arguing with Robbie even more.

July 2006 came, and we went to Fort Lauderdale on our annual summer vacation at the beach, a place Robbie had only gone once; he never dared to go back. For the first time in a few years, I was totally engaged with both children.

That trip was especially difficult. It was the first time in a couple of years that I was away from home for about ten days straight. I was getting used to not traveling and being home more. Nevertheless, I focused on making my children happy.

I could not reach Robbie once on the phone. He would not pick up either the cell or the home phone, and would not return any messages. I was truly concerned more about his welfare than the welfare of the marriage at this point.

When we came back home, Robbie had deteriorated much more. He looked drunk or high all the time. He was constantly in the barn or at the back by the lake. His brother Ramchand and his wife were planning to come to Florida and wanted to visit us the following week. Robbie absolutely did not want anyone to come to the home anymore. It did not matter who. He had become and wanted us to become more and more isolated; it was stifling me little by little. I did not give in or give up anymore. I was fighting for my life at this point. I wanted his brother to visit. I wanted people back at the house. I wanted to enjoy life once again. I wanted peace and happiness within me and within my home. I could not change what happened in the past, but I could certainly change what I did next.

A week went by after we got back. Robbie and I did not talk to or even look at each other. The following weekend rolled around. Ramchand called on Saturday and said he was on the Florida Turnpike on the way to visit us. I told Robbie and he went nuts. He told me to call back and tell them not to come. I was calm. We were in the barn. He paced back and forth, agitated. He yelled at me to get out and call them back. His yelling and swearing at me was finally causing me to become agitated and disgusted. I calmly walked over and tossed his stereo way across the barn. He would fiddle with this stereo each time I tried to talk with him. It broke to pieces. That felt really good! I told him to do what he wanted to do, as it no longer mattered to me. I told him I would tell his brother about our sorry life. I went into the house and continued with my chores.

I was trying really hard to calm down. I kept busy and blasted the stereo that was in the house. I needed a distraction, as fear was starting to build up again. I did not need fear; I needed strength and encouragement. Music was a good distraction for me.

My cell phone suddenly rang. It was Robbie calling me from outside. He said he was getting the f— out of there and that his brother could go f— himself. He left. Ramchand arrived a few minutes later. He wanted to know where Robbie had gone. I said I didn't know. I lied and did not tell them anything. They stayed a short while, and I knew they felt bad, but I still wanted to hide what was going on.

That was a bad summer for Robbie. His health and weight were probably at their lowest. He was extremely skinny, I believe around a hundred thirty-eight pounds—probably thirty pounds underweight for his height and body mass. I also noticed him talking to himself a lot. We would be sitting in the living room, trying not to even breathe hard since it could set him off. It hurts me to this day to think our children could not be comfortable in their home at the most critical times in their young lives. Robbie would have a conversation by himself and motion with his hands a lot. To witness this was painful for me. I was sure he was becoming mentally ill.

I did not know at the time that he had a form of mental illness resulting from alcoholism.

I called Robbie's brother Kumar that year and asked if anyone on their side of the family ever had a nervous breakdown. He said no one had that he was aware of. I told him briefly my concerns about Robbie's unusual behavior. He was somewhat concerned, but I had the feeling he did not want to get involved, as it could cause issues with Robbie and me. I told him to let the rest of Robbie's family know I'd called with concerns. By then I had ruled out any issues between Robbie and me. Robbie had issues, not me. I was sure of that.

Finally, 2006 ended. I made a decision, a decision I never thought I would have made even a few months ago. I did not know at the time whether it was a right or a wrong decision, but I reflected on what Mahatma Gandhi once said: "You may never know what results come of your actions, but if you do nothing there will be no result." I decided I would have a discussion with Robbie and clearly lay out my plan so there was no confusion on his part. We sat outside. I told him I needed to speak with him and that I did not want to argue. I told him that when I was done, I would let him know and he could then have time to say what he wanted.

I told him that I knew for sure I was not contributing to his behavior. I declared to him that I had stayed out of it for a year, and I was willing to give him another year to try to fix whatever was wrong. I was here to help in any way, but I would not be contributing to any arguments. If he had nothing good to discuss with me, he should not speak to me. I mentioned I was getting older and was finding it harder and harder to manage my life with the current confusion and the emotional and verbal abuse. I could no longer work and take care of the home and children. He ought to help me more. I couldn't keep mowing the lawn or doing repairs and maintenance by myself.

By this time, Robbie was working little and only working in the garden. It got him out of the house. He did nothing else. I was getting more and more tired of trying to cover all the odd jobs around the house and taking care of his business activities, his banking, bills, and general activities associated with a small business.

I volunteered to show him how to manage his business and told him he could do his banking and anything else he needed to do. I would continue to do his business taxes. I would answer any questions or even help him at times when I had the energy, but I could no longer do his job as well as mine. I was here to help him if he needed me to guide him to see a doctor or a counselor. I would stand in support of him if he tried to fix his issues. I did not know what his problems were, as he had not spoken to me in over a year. I told him I loved him and probably always would to some extent, but I was making a decision that day to give this marriage another year. If by the end of 2007 he had not made any improvements, I would file for a divorce and end the marriage. This decision I needed to make for me. I told him I was not doing it for any reason other than to get the children and me out of the terrible situation he had put us in. I promised I was not going to destroy my life because he did not place any value on his own life, but I was getting out of the sinking ship of a marriage and taking my children with me. Robbie simply sat there, and when I was done, I asked if he had anything to say.

"No," he said.

He got up and left. I felt like a burden had been lifted from my heart. I was sure he wanted out of the marriage at that moment, and I had made it easy for him to walk away. I sat on the swing and the tears rolled down my cheeks.

I am human, and for this reason, I am expected to be humane. In spite of the fact that someone else may cause me extreme pain and sorrow, I ought to still treat them with respect, fairness, and dignity as much as I can without endangering my life or the lives of others.

An Unforgettable Start to 2007

Some events in life may be predictable, but most come as a surprise.

In early 2007, I started seeking professional counseling. For the first time in my life, I had to let others in my family know what was happening. I told Lakhram, Devika, and my nephew, Vic. I asked for them to listen to me, as I desperately needed others to talk with. That January I went over to Devika's in Orlando and told her not to come back to my home. I told her I would visit her at her home if we needed to get together, but this year I wanted all my family to stay away from my home, as I wanted to give Robbie a good chance of making a change in his life. It pained me to tell her not to come to my home. She was a single mom, and she loved coming over with her children to visit me, yet I had to look her in the eye and tell her not to visit me anymore. Devika asked if I was seeing a counselor, and that week I called and made an appointment. My privacy was no longer of importance, however, saving my life and the lives of my children became my number one priority.

I asked Robbie to come with me to the appointment but he refused. He told me to shove the counselor up my ass. I started to see the counselor anyway, and he started to help me get my emotions under control. He told me that from his experience, this marriage had some serious issues, and if Robbie refused to go to counseling, there was nothing I could do the fix this. I started to think seriously about the possibility of a divorce and the reality of it, something I knew I was prepared to do to save the three of us, Sam, Randy, and me.

I remember telling Robbie sometime during the year that I would support him, but I would not go out in the *storm* with him. This was extremely painful. I loved this man; how could I walk away? I had to choose between his life and ours. I chose the latter, regardless of what my emotional state was and would be. By now, it was going on five years of immense turmoil. This was a long time to watch the relationship spiral downward. I was finally learning how to manage my emotions and not ignore them. I was learning to face adversity with grace and dignity, never with anger. I was growing up slowly.

Randy, Sam, and I went off to Canada that spring for ten days. When we came back, Robbie was at his worst. He was literally behaving like a madman. He would walk back and forth, in and out of the house, talking to himself and arguing with no one. I then made the painful decision early that summer of 2007 to leave him since I couldn't reach him any longer and he refused all the help I offered. I had run out of options.

At this point, I started talking to Lakhram and a few of Robbie's friends about Robbie's behavior. I remember going to dinner at the house of a friend of his, and I completely broke down and started crying. This had never happened before. I had to let it out or else this secret life would eventually take a toll on me. Robbie's friends were shocked to find out this had been happening for years. They were shocked to know things were that bad. They also tried to talk to Robbie. He was never willing to listen to anything they had to say.

I continued to see my counselor. I was starting to develop the strength I needed to go through with the divorce. I could not have done it without the help of those who really had my concerns at heart. No one told me what to do. They helped me get stronger emotionally and deal with the possibility of being alone after twenty-one years of marriage and a twenty-six-year relationship with the person I loved.

However, I got to choose now how and whom I wanted in my life. I no longer would give my life and love away for nothing in return. I had two decades with a person who did not care about me or about my feelings. I had to protect myself and my children at all cost, even at the sacrifice of my marriage and possibly Robbie. I used to panic at the thought of being alone and without a partner. I guess even though Robbie was not there for me, he was still a partner. I was fearful of being alone and of being unable to find a person to share the rest of my life with.

It was June 2007. Randy was in New York, and Sam was at a friend's house spending two weeks of summer vacation. I told no one what I planned to do. I decided that when both children were out of the house, I would get an attorney and have Robbie served with divorce papers. This way, if he became violent, my children would not be in any danger. I was willing to take that risk knowing it could cost me my life. I was ready. Emotionally, I was feeling a lot of pain and sadness—there was some fear, but with the help of my counselor, my brother, sister, and my writing, I was able to keep my emotions under control and focus on what I needed to do.

Robbie was drunk every day. I took a few days off and went to North Carolina for a much-needed mental rest to get my head together. When I came back, Robbie was not home. It was Father's Day of 2007. No one was able to reach him. His friends called his cell phone repeatedly with no answer. I called several times with no answer either. I finally received a call from him around 5:00 p.m. He was swearing and yelling, asking why I wanted to know where the f— he was at. He said he did not give a f— and when he got home he would end it all since that was what I wanted. He was becoming physically threatening himself. As I was writing this, I tried hard to remember how I was feeling at the time, but I did not journal a lot on my feelings, so I cannot remember. I was journaling more on what I did and what he did. In the beginning, I wrote a lot about my feelings and my sadness, but I wish I had written more later on about my feelings and thoughts versus so much about the events. I strongly believe now I had to block my pain in order to gain strength and courage.

When Robbie moved to threatening suicide, I realized I could not help him any longer and needed to focus on my safety and the safety of Randy and Sam. This madness was now taking another weird turn. I packed a suitcase and left my home. I did not plan on ever coming back. I would get an attorney and find a place to stay until the divorce was final. My decision was made.

I was now seeing the counselor twice a week, as my emotions were raw and I was starting to cry a lot more. I was also talking to Lakhram and Devika a lot more. They were my emotional rocks. God bless them. They both stayed away from giving me advice. The decision to leave Robbie was my own decision. No one else had a part in that decision.

I went to a friend's house that night, then got up and went to work on Monday. I did not call Robbie, nor did I answer the phone when he called repeatedly. The first thing I did was to look up an attorney. I made an appointment for a counseling session. I paid a fee of $375 that would be applied to the total cost of a divorce in the event I retained their services.

I booked a hotel for a week until I decided where I wanted to rent an apartment. It was a Tuesday evening, after Father's Day, when Robbie called again and I decided to answer. Here is a recap of a disturbing one-sided conversation from Robbie.

"You better get home and get Sam home now. If not you are going to find me dead in the barn," he blurted out.

I started to shake. I was losing control of my emotions. I wanted to run home and stop the divorce. I did not want to face the possibility of the death of my children's father. I was crying in my car as I sat there motionless. I was, starting to visualize all this in my head. I was also starting to take responsibility for Robbie's act of ending his own life. I was tremendously scared and said to myself that I should not have left our home. I kept saying to myself I was the cause of it all. I told him I was on my way home and started driving aimlessly to get home as quickly as I could. I called Devika. She calmed me down and brought me back to a reality.

Finally, it dawned on me: if I got home and he was dead or was waiting to hurt me, was I prepared? The answer was no. I needed to stand up for myself and ensure my safety. I realized I'd had a moment of weakness and needed to recover quickly. Talking to another person helped me focus on my priorities. I called 911 and asked to be transferred to the Lake County Sheriff's office. I made a report of an attempted suicide and updated them on what had happened and what had led up to this. They advised me not to go home but to wait for them at the outskirts of town and an officer would come escort me. I hadn't waited long before I saw two officers go to the house; then one came to get me. I drove behind him down the driveway, not knowing what I would see on the other end. The feeling of not being able to do anything to help Robbie was overwhelming. I simply could not think beyond that moment. I could not imagine what I would do if he were to end his life. What would I tell Randy and Sam? Would they blame me forever? Would they hate me forever?

The officers had entered the home and found Robbie sitting quietly in the living room with a glazed look on his face. One of the officers told me that my husband seemed "mentally deranged," was lacking focus, and unable to answer simple questions. He seemed calm and out of reality. They knew he was drunk. They spoke to both of us and told Robbie to take a shower and get to bed; if they had to come back, they would take him to jail. Robbie calmly agreed. The officers left, but they were not even at the end of the driveway when Robbie flung his dinner plate in the kitchen. It broke to pieces. He started swearing and saying again he was going to the barn to kill himself. I dialed 911 and the officers came back immediately. This time, they told me I had the right to "Baker Act" Robbie. This was the first time I learned that if another family member was suicidal or acting threateningly because of alcohol consumption or drugs, as the sane spouse or family member I had the right to send him to a lockdown facility for recovery.

I was happy I had this option. Finally, I had learned of a place that he could go to get the kind of help I could not give. They handcuffed Robbie and explained to him what was happening. I signed the documentation, and Robbie was off to Lifestream Behavioral Center in Leesburg. I was relieved. I slept well knowing he was in capable hands and could not harm himself or me.

I researched online what this facility did; for the first time, I was educating myself on symptoms of addictions. I was up late reading. I was now sure that once Robbie realized he actually had a problem, he would, of course, fix his problem. He would realize that I loved him and would really try hard. You'd think that would be what he would do.

I called Robbie's brother Kumar and told him what had happened, hoping that Robbie's family would start to support him. I was still seeing a counselor and talking to Lakhram and Devika for emotional support. I had to be strong. I had learned a lot over the years not to react to a situation where I had no control.

I left for a family reunion in New York that week while Robbie was at the behavioral center. The day of my trip, I met with one of the counselors at Lifestream along with Robbie. It was an open discussion. Robbie was shaking and crying a lot. I was nervous. I told the counselor that Robbie had emotionally and verbally abused me for a long time, and that I'd made the decision I was not going to live that way any longer. My message was clear to Robbie: he needed to change or I was leaving him. I had little else to say. I took Sam and got on a plane to New York.

When I started talking to others about my issues and problems, I immediately began to feel some relief. I think it's because other people are outside of my painful environment and have no motive but to help. I also was able to see my life in a different light, as if I were looking into myself from the outside. I leaned on others and drew strength, courage, and hope to go on.

Post Baker Act

*No one else is the cause of our troubles; we
are the architects of our own destinies.*

At my family reunion I told no one what had happened. Only Lakhram knew, and he advised me to share my situation with Puchie and Shammie in case something happened to Robbie while I was gone. Robbie was scheduled to be released from the clinic while I was in New York. I had individual conversations with them both and for the first time told them I was having issues with Robbie and that he was not doing well. I did not go much into the details. They both told me to do what I needed to do for myself and for my children.

I returned home the day after Robbie was released from the clinic. He was not at home when Sam and I arrived. About an hour later, he came in. Sam and I were in the living room. As soon as Robbie entered the living room, he began swearing and blaming me for his having to spend time in the clinic. He was in a rage. I was starting to get scared. I was concerned about Sam and for what she was feeling. I did not want a confrontation, so I did not say one word. I simply picked up my purse and drove to the Lake County Courthouse to speak to a domestic violence counselor in the district attorney's office. The Lake County sheriff's office had given this information when Robbie was Baker Acted. Robbie called me numerous times and asked where I was going. I told him I was going to get a restraining order to protect our children and me from him.

When I was in the room with the domestic violence counselor, I received a call from Robbie's brother Kumar. He asked me as a personal favor not to proceed with the restraining order. I really liked Robbie's little brother and felt sad for him and his family, so I decided to leave without filing the order. The domestic violence representative must have seen this before—women giving up at the last minute. I was no different.

From what I understood, Robbie had told his brother that he was going to change. That was all I needed to hear. A mere glimpse of hope was enough to make me reconsider my actions. I drove back home with my heart full of hope that Robbie was seeing the light and would change. I believe now I wanted to stay married so badly I would have hung on to any promise, even an empty one.

As I pulled out of the courthouse, I realized I had left Sam in the house with Robbie in a rage! My heart was racing. The car was not going fast enough to make it home. How could I not think of how I'd left my child behind with her dad in a mad rage? I was extremely scared for my daughter's safety and wondered how she was feeling. I should have not left her. This was a mistake. I ran into the house looking for Sam. She was sleeping soundly on her bed. I was relieved, but I should have taken her with me. Then I left to find Robbie.

Robbie was sitting quietly in the barn. I knelt down in front of him and held his hands and said I would stand by him; whatever I needed to do I would do. I told him I would go get the prescriptions the clinic recommended and set up the counselor's appointment. I would even go with him if he wanted me to. He was agreeable, and we stood up and gave each other a warm and loving hug. Finally, I was feeling blessed; he was going to make this change! I thought at the time God was answering my prayers. I left with Sam to go to the drug store. The prescriptions were twelve hundred dollars, and I had to pay my portion of two hundred and eighty-five dollars. I was happy and hopeful, as I was sure this was the end of years of madness.

When I returned to the barn, I was shocked to see that within the hour it took me to go to the drugstore and back, Robbie had gone through a metamorphosis. He was no longer quiet and agreeable. He was as mad as a raging tornado. As soon as I entered the barn, he started swearing and accusing me of putting him in this situation, again! I was the cause of all his problems, and now he had to take medication that the "no good" doctors thought he needed. He stood up and raised his right hand as if to hit me across the face or head area. I blocked his hand and backed off outside of this reach. I was mad and hurt. Not sure what to do next, I started to turn around and was about to go back in the house. Robbie sat back down on the chair. As I was about to exit the barn, I completely lost it. I turned around, walked up to the chair, and kicked it so hard it flew to the other side of the barn with him in it.

I quickly walked over to him, looked down at him, and said, "Don't you ever try to hit me again. I don't care anymore. Go do what you want to do. I am over this!"

I went into the house. I gave up. As promised, I got the prescriptions and planned make the appointments with the counselors regardless of my personal feelings of disappointment. Not five minutes later, Robbie came storming into the house and showed me clearly he had no concerns about my feelings, his feelings, or anyone else's. He opened all the prescription bottles I had purchased and dumped each one into the garbage. Twelve hundred dollars down the garbage. Yes, that was how he was going to fix himself.

It is my opinion the promises made by addicts more often than not cannot be fulfilled if they are still active. I believe they mean well, but they are battling powerful forces within themselves to which they succumb time and time again. Those who are able to stop drinking and maintain sobriety earn my utmost respect.

Test of Faith

Egoism and pride could be the beginning of our ruin.

It was late June 2007. As promised, I made the appointments with the counselors. I gave Robbie the information. You guessed it, he never showed up for any of the appointments. At this point, I was more concerned about returning to where I had been emotionally, fearing that the recovery and strength I had gained might be lost again. I was working double time to stay focused. I was not drinking and focused on the children and myself. Each time I had the urge to drink or knock myself out, I would focus on the birth of both Randy and Sam. Those two special moments in my life made me want to work even harder at recovering. They deserved a better mom. I would be that mom someday, but not yet. I had to get better first.

Robbie decided to take the summer off from work. As the days and weeks went by, we were starting to talk to each other again a little, and his behavior was starting to improve as well. I purchased vitamins, supplements, shakes, and whatever I thought would help him gain weight back. He was extremely thin and looked unhealthy and unkempt. He was eating very little. I would remind him each day to drink the Ensure shakes, to take his vitamins, and to keep going to his doctor.

I really wanted him to get better and I really wanted it to work out, but not at the cost of my sanity. I'd never wanted a divorce, even though I knew this was not the marriage I wanted either. My sense of loyalty to the vows I took meant a lot to me. It saddened me each time I thought what my life would be if I were to lose the marriage. I knew I would miss it a lot. I would miss Robbie's presence and being in a marriage even though it was not much of a marriage at this stage or at any stage. I feared the thought of being single and alone. There were times when I was willing to risk my health, my life, and my children's lives for Robbie. At this point, I was not in love with him anymore. All those years of emotional torture finally took a toll on me. However, I was not angry or mean to him. I really wanted to help him get better, but definitely not at the cost of my life.

The summer finally ended. I was continuing to see a counselor, and Robbie and I were getting along better. We were talking, going places, and I could see a drastic difference in his behavior. September rolled around, and I remember meeting Robbie for lunch after one of my counseling appointments in Orlando. It was starting to rain slightly. At that session, my counselor asked me to invite Robbie, thinking maybe he could join us and we could try to work things out. I was happy to hear this and was excited to ask Robbie. Things were going well, and I was sure he would want to go. At lunch I asked, and without hesitation, he again told me to shove the counselor up my ass! It was downhill for me after that conversation. Robbie said he could do this on his own and did not need anyone to tell him what to do or how to do it. He had tried in years past, but his efforts lasted only a few months, not much longer, and then he was back to his old behaviors. I had seen this dozens of times. I also knew that if the behaviors came back, it would finally break me. I would have to make a drastic decision to save my sanity.

My mind was starting to race as I wondered if Robbie was pretending to want this to work out or was truly into saving our marriage. I was crying and confused all the way back to work. It was raining slightly, and I was not focusing a lot on my driving. My mind was all over the place. Suddenly, I lost control of my Toyota Camry as I was exiting to get to work. I briefly remember the car spinning out of control and slamming into the guardrails, spinning some more, and hitting the guardrails again. I ended up sitting in the middle of the exit. The car was crushed, front and back, with me in the middle. I was not injured, but I was frazzled and shaken.

This happens to us when our mind wonders about things that we have little control over. I could not allow myself to be maimed, injured, or worse, dead. I had to refocus on myself. I could not help those who did not want to help themselves, namely Robbie. I felt he did not value his life, my life, or the children's lives enough to want to make a change; even sadder, he did not have the ability or strength to make the change. Yet he did not want any help from me or anyone else. I felt helpless, it was maddening.

After the accident, Robbie again started to behave better. He went regularly to his doctor, and during one of his visits, his doctor found some alarming results. Robbie was referred to the cancer center at Dr. Phillips Hospital. This was a real scare for both of us. Nevertheless, I stayed serene and hoped for the best. After a series of tests, we finally saw the cancer doctor. He told us Robbie had a condition called thalassemia trait where his red blood cells were smaller than normal; he had to be careful about his diet and consumption of alcohol. We were relieved. This was a scare no family wanted to endure, but by the grace of God, Robbie did not have any life-threatening illness.

For the few months from September to November 2007 as we were going through this, Robbie focused on his health. He was now back to 165 pounds from 138 a few months back. I was extremely happy. He was looking healthy again.

Our last visit to the cancer doctor was November 17, 2007, when Robbie was 165 pounds. A few weeks later, he came out of the bathroom in his underwear, and I noticed he was really skinny. I asked how much he weighed and he said 165. I could not believe he was 165 by the looks of him. I took him back to the scale and told him to step on it. Robbie was 152 pounds. Ten days after November 17, Robbie had lost thirteen pounds! What was wrong with him? Was he not eating? I told him he could not come this far and let himself go again. This was not what he wanted to hear. He was very angry and said the doctors, including his primary physician, were a bunch of "assholes" who did not know what they were doing.

Arguing with Robbie was useless. I was convinced he was drinking heavily again on a daily basis. I learned the hard way to stay out and keep the focus on me and on my health.

I was starting to wonder when this madness would end. When would Robbie wake up and take charge of his life? When would he care enough to want to not hurt those he was supposed to love or, even worse, when would he hurt himself? I was now starting to become detached from his problems more and more with each passing day. The year of counseling was really helping me focus on my problems and get the energy to work and take care of the children. Randy and Sam needed me more than ever now. I was the only parent they could talk to or trust. This was sad. Their dad used to be a good and engaging dad. He never was a good husband, but he had been a good dad up until a few years ago. I had been willing to give up my happiness and lack of fulfillment in the marriage as long as the children were happy. I sacrificed a lot for family. I hoped someday they would thank me for it.

November rolled into December. Little did I know December 2007 would be the beginning of new turmoil I was unprepared for.

In my experience, counseling went a long way in helping me face the reality of the complex situation. I feel counselors are specially trained professionals who are there to help those willing to help themselves. My hat's off to them.

My Darkest Days

It is our right to defend ourselves.

It was Saturday, December 8, 2007. Robbie was going to a funeral in Orlando. It was like any normal Saturday around the house with chores, working in the yard, and other weekend work. The funeral was at 10:00 a.m. Around 8:00 a.m. Robbie and I washed and vacuumed the Honda Accord, the car he was going to the funeral in. It was a pleasant morning, no arguments, just two people working together. Robbie said after the funeral he was going to the supermarket and would get something to fix for lunch. I was happy since Saturday was my house-cleaning day. At least I could clean house and not worry about lunch. My husband would take care of that. He left around 9:00 a.m.

Lunchtime came and went. Dinnertime came and went. No Robbie. He would not answer his cell phone and he never called home. By now, I was getting used to him not letting me know where he was and not answering his phone. For all the years we were married, he would never truly tell me where he went and rarely came home when he promised. I gave up on that years ago. I knew if I asked, it would lead to huge argument. By now, I went nowhere with him, not even the grocery store. No parties, no social gatherings, nowhere, period. I was tired of being the wife for show only. I wanted a real marriage with a real person who loved and cared for me and who wanted to be there with me. That was all I wanted. Nothing else mattered to me.

As I became older, I realized that in order to love another, one has to think of the other person first. Based on this definition, some people cannot truly love others, in my opinion. Robbie never loved me; he loved being married to me, but did not love me. Why could I not have love? What had I done that was wrong to have deserved this person in my life? I questioned everything I ever did in the marriage, trying to find faults in myself. I did not find much except that I let him walk around without having to compromise or apologize. I should have stood up for my dignity much, much sooner than this.

Finally, at 8:00 p.m. Robbie came home. Randy, Sam, and I were in my room on the bed watching a movie. Robbie walked in and saw us. I said hello to him, and he looked at us and calmly walked back out of the room. Around 8:30 p.m. I told Randy to go feed the dogs. I was starting to get a little scared. I did not like the look on Robbie's face when he came into the room. I was trying to keep the children quiet and close and pray Robbie would have dinner and go to bed; then it would be one more day over and the next day would start again. I did not want any outbursts, swearing, or arguing. Randy went outside, got the dog bowls, and went into the garage to fill the bowls up. I perked up my ears, as I needed to be aware of where Robbie was. I was not feeling good and had a gut feeling he was looking for a fight. I knew I would not give in to him this time for sure. I was prepared mentally to deal with anything at this point. Remember, it was my life I was fighting to save, not his.

I suddenly heard talking in the living room. Robbie asked Randy to show him the dog bowls. That was all I heard, and then the back door opened and Randy went out to put out the dog food. Randy came back straight to the bedroom as instructed and got back in bed to my right as we continued watching the movie. I was focusing little at that point on the movie. All was too quiet. Something was brewing. Suddenly, Robbie stormed into the bedroom.

"Your son shoved dog food in my face when I was eating. Is that how you raised him? You are teaching him really good," he said sarcastically.

There was no question in my mind that Robbie was lying. Nevertheless, he was pacing back and forth, and he looked like a lunatic. It was the look I had seen earlier when he came into the room. He was furiously twitching his hands together, walking back and forth, and swearing a lot. I never opened my mouth. I was scared to death. I was shaking.

"I need to get the f— out of here. I have had enough of this shit. Give me ten thousand dollars and I want to get the f— out. I can't stand this f—ing place anymore. I want to go to Guyana and live. I do not want this shit anymore. I want to leave," he said.

What had happened between nine this morning and eight tonight? I was confused at this point and felt helpless. I felt both Randy and Sam becoming tense next to me. I had to do something now, but what?

I simply said, "Well, Robbie, there are four exits to take. Pick any one you like and go. I really do not give a shit which one. If that's what you want, knock yourself out."

I meant every word. In past years I was not strong to stand up to him. I was getting stronger each day. One day at a time. He left the room for a brief moment and stormed back in.

"This is it, I am going to get the f—ing gun and end it all once and for all," he threatened.

Did that mean kill us or kill himself? What should I do? My head was spinning faster and faster. I looked at the children; they both had the comforter pulled up to their chins and were shaking, especially Sam. This broke my heart into a million pieces. They had not bargained for this when they came into this world. They were innocent victims of a terrible marriage and a madman for a dad. Randy was shaking, and I was unsure what emotions were going through his mind. Every vein on his right arm was popping out as he had formed a tight fist. I felt Randy was moments from springing off the bed toward his dad. He was struggling to control himself. Robbie left the room. I heard the front door open and close. Was he going to get the gun from the barn? I had to do something. I looked at Randy and asked,

"Should I call the cops?"

Why was I asking a kid what to do? What was I thinking?

"Do whatever you want, Mom," he said.

What was wrong with me? Why was I asking a fifteen-year-old what to do? I was the adult, I should know what to do. What kind of mother was I if I could not protect my own children? This was the point in my life where I decided that at all costs I would protect them. No one, not even their dad, would ever threaten their lives as long as I was alive and breathing. I would stand strong for them until the day I died. They were my responsibility, and I had never run from my responsibilities. I would not run now. I would stand up and stand firm, even if I were left standing alone.

I picked up the house phone and dialed 911. By now, the sheriff's office knew the situation, and as soon as they saw the phone number, they were on their way. I heard the front door open and close again. I prayed, *God, please help me this one last time. Please don't let him come in here with the gun, please, please God. I will never ask for anything else in my whole life. I prayed like I have never prayed before. One last favor, God, one last favor, please help me. I swear this is it.* I closed my eyes tightly shut.

Robbie did not come into the room. I was shaking. In about three minutes I heard the dogs barking, which was a sure sign the officers were pulling in. I had them on the phone, and they told me to stay exactly where I was and not move. I heard the front door open again. I heard conversations. They were in the house. I saw a flashlight on the back porch. I saw one of them walk into the bedroom. I took my first breath in what felt like ten minutes. I was finally relieved.

Another officer came into the room. He asked me to go outside with him while the other one stayed with Randy and Sam. As I was walking outside, I saw Robbie sitting on the sofa with dinner and an officer standing in front of him. I started to cry. Robbie had not gotten the gun. Was I doing the right thing? Would there be a next time? Would he get the gun then? What risks was I willing to take until it was too late? When would it be too late? When was it time to stand up for my children and me? Was there such a thing as the right time? No, there is no such thing as the right time, only what we feel at the moment and with the actions at that moment. That was all I had. Thoughts were flowing so fast, I felt like I was going to pass out.

The officer started to question me about the incident. I spoke truly as to the details of what happened. I was not willing to lie to protect Robbie if my children's lives were in danger. I wrote in my handwriting what had happened, swore, and signed the document. The other officer came out after speaking to both Randy and Sam. He called the one I was talking with and they chatted for about five minutes. They both came back to me, and said the children's version was the same as mine and they had no reason to doubt Robbie had threatened us. This was a serious matter. I was outside about thirty minutes or so, and the whole time I was crying and wondering what Randy and Sam were doing in my room and what they were thinking. I wanted to be with them so badly it was painful. I wanted to hold them, to tell them everything would be OK, and that this too shall pass. I wanted to do all those things, yet here I was standing outside, alone, shaking and crying. I wanted to vomit.

Finally, the front door opened and Robbie was escorted in handcuffs. He was placed in the backseat of the cruiser. The officer that took him came up to me and said, "I am arresting your husband under the Baker Act. I believe he is under the influence of some substance. At this time, he is not coherent and cannot answer simple questions. From my experience, he is either drunk or on drugs. I am not sure. I do not feel this warrants an arrest for domestic violence. He is incapable of talking, and I simply have no other choice but to Baker Act him and place him in the care of Lifestream again."

I was breathing a lot better. There were three police cars, and a local officer came in as well. One went into the barn, one went into the garage at home, one went out back, and one came into the house. After Robbie was taken away, a couple of them stayed and provided me information on how to safely lock up the guns. They gave me the name and a number of the local gun shop that would give me free locks. They also told me I should consider getting my own handgun to protect myself, as I was all the way out there alone. Finally, they told me that since they had been out several times and there were minors in the home, it was possible I might receive a call from the Department of Children and Family. I was advised about the steps I needed to take to ensure the safety of my children; if not the State of Florida would have no choice but to step in and possibly remove the children from a home that could be deemed unsafe.

I was sure this would never happen. I was able to protect my children and keep them away from harm. I did not want them to be further displaced than they already were. I wanted to make life for them as normal as possible and attempt to mend those parts of their young lives that might have already been damaged.

That week I went to Peterson's Gun shop in Eustis, Florida, and obtained the locks for the shotguns we had in the home. I also applied for clearance and purchased a personal handgun for myself with a locked case as well. I took a course on gun safety and usage. I was scared and nervous, as my life was now taking a course I was unprepared for. However, I was starting to understand the consequences of abuse and to expect the unexpected. Safety for my children and me became a primary concern. I took extra measures to educate my children on gun safety as well. Growing up in the country as they had, owning a gun was a normal practice. However, it was necessary to ensure they were trained properly on the importance of guns and the danger they represented.

A few weeks later, I upgraded the ADT security system to add monitoring cameras around the home as added security. I installed a few Web cameras to view my home from anywhere using a basic Internet connection. By setting my TV to an auxiliary channel, I was also able to see when anyone entered my property.

However, before I did any of this, I took steps I should have taken a long time ago. I took legal action against Robbie.

I should have not waited until my abusive relationship reached a point where I was in terrible fear for my life. I should have been more alert and assertive in seeking out some solutions to prevent the escalation.

S.T.O.P.

Our actions have many ramifications on those around us; therefore, let them be noble.

The next morning came as sure as I expected. What would I do first? Ironically, my head was clear as to what I needed to do. My Higher Power works miracles in so many ways. He cleared my head overnight.

I called Puchie in New York and asked her to contact Robbie's parents and let them know what happened. I told her to ask them to come and support him if they wanted to. Next, I called Robbie's eldest brother, Ramchand. I had not spoken with Ramchand in over a year. I was nervous but empowered, as I was finally doing what I should have done years before. Nevertheless, I spoke slowly and clearly. Ramchand was furious at first and handed the phone to his wife, who was much calmer. I briefly related what had happened in the past few years and told them to call their younger brother, Kumar, who was aware of what had happened.

Next, I sent Randy and Sam off to school and got dressed. Devika was leaving for Orlando and relocating to Canada for a few years. I knew if I called her, she would not leave. I was unwilling to take this risk, so I sat and cried, as I was not able to call her and tell her. I really needed her or any family at that point. I felt alone. At that time, I really thought I was alone and that no one would understand or be able to help me. I was wrong. I would find out later if I had only talked about my situation to others, people would have truly wanted to help me.

I want my readers to learn these things if they find themselves in a similar situation. I wished I had trusted some of my closest friends more. Maybe it would have made the pain a little less. I had to learn the hard way because I chose that. I was ignorant and inexperienced.

It was about 9:00 a.m. on Monday. I got in my car and went to the Lake County Courthouse to the district attorney's office, where I asked to speak to the same representative I had walked away from back in June. I told her I would like to file an injunction (a restraining order) against my husband for domestic violence. She took his name and pulled data from the Lake County database. By then, I assumed the incident from the night before was already in the system. It was, and she gave me paperwork to complete and asked me to be as truthful as possible. I never planned to do otherwise. I was serene and at peace by now. I knew I was doing the right thing. I had no remorse or second guesses as to what I was about to do. It was a beautiful feeling. For the first time in twenty years, I was telling another person, a stranger, about the physical abuse when Robbie hit me the first year. I planned to start from the beginning. I left the district attorney's office after swearing to what I had written. I was given a copy of the injunction order and was told Robbie would be served at Lifestream Behavioral Center that day sometime before 5:00 p.m.

I called my office and told my boss I was going to be late. I called the attorney I had a retained back in June and said I needed to see them at 10:00 a.m. I reiterated what had happened and gave them copies of the injunction order. Then they asked me a question I already knew the answer to.

"Are you going to file for dissolution of the marriage?"

"Yes" was my firm and confident response.

There was no need to ponder, think, or question my decision. My mind was made up. This would end one way or another. I was no longer planning to live in sadness and fear. Life had to be better than this. I was not angry but decisive. Making decisions as a business leader was easy. This should be no different. This was a decision that I had to make, and I was the only one who could make it. I was the only one who knew that if I did not get out, I was placing my children's lives in danger. I did not want them to ask me in later years why I did not stand up for my dignity. I wanted to lead by example. I wanted them to emulate what was right. We all have the ability to stand up for ourselves. I wish my family had been there to help me at that critical time. It would have been a lot easier.

I signed the necessary paperwork and paid the attorney's fee. Then I left for my office. It was about 11:30 a.m. I went to work and to my boss's office and asked to speak with him and his boss. I asked for the door to be closed. Until that point, no one from my work knew of the years of unhappiness I was going through. I was performing well at work and I controlled

S.T.O.P.

my emotions and mood when I was there. I was able to separate work from home. It was hard, but I needed my job to keep me sane because home was where insanity existed.

I thought I was strong and would get through this without problems or emotions. I was wrong. I was not prepared for what was about to happen. The moment the door closed, I crashed. I had lost my will to talk. Our vice president came up to me and gave me a hug. I think she knew I needed that. You have no idea how badly I needed a hug. The reality of what had transpired so far came crashing down on me. Finally, I was able to compose myself and spoke as slowly as I could.

"I want to let you both know that I am going through a rough time and have been for a few years now. I am going through with a divorce. I have made my decision and I wanted to let you know. I will need time away from the office during the days ahead to take care of legal issues. My attorney is ten minutes away, and I need to be able to run over there at a moment's notice. I want you to know that I will be in and out of the office the next few weeks," I said.

I did not need to explain any further. They understood and did not question my request. I respect both of them for not asking me anything. I was not prepared to say anything else. They told me to take whatever time I needed and they were there for me. I needed their support more than ever. I went back to my desk and proceeded to make a series of phone calls.

I first called Lakhram and told him what had happened. I called Puchie back to ensure she had spoken to Robbie's parents; she had. I called the clinic at Lifestream to find out how Robbie was doing. I was given no information since I was not the one who Baker Acted him; hence, I had no authorization. This was fine with me. For once, I was not going to clean up the mess Robbie has gotten himself into. I was a little relieved. Finally, I called my counselor and we talked over the phone. I needed to let a person independent of the situation know how I felt. Speaking to an independent counselor was one of the best decisions I had made to save my sanity.

I began my workday sometime after noon. I tried as best as I could to focus on work and not on my emotions. If I did, I would get in my car, go back, and undo all I had done that morning. I would not be able to separate myself from Robbie, the one person I wanted to spend the rest of my life with. I would go to the clinic to get him out. I might have even admitted I made a big mistake. It was safe not to focus on my emotions. Those emotions would cause me to do things that were not right. I had to do this or else it would destroy my children's lives. Sam was already starting to stay in her room and wouldn't come out for hours. I think now she was scared all the time. Randy was starting to show some serious anger. I am so sorry that I did not focus on them as much as I should. I had to save my children from this total madness. I kept repeating this mantra to myself that morning.

The day ended, and I drove home as fast as I could to be with Randy and Sam. We went out to dinner to talk and so I could update them on my decision and the next steps. They sat and listened, but did not say much. I was sure they were happy the madness was finally coming to an end. I could see the relief on both their faces. They did not have to be afraid anymore. I told them I would be there for them and that they could trust I was doing the right thing. I did not cry. I did not want them to see me showing signs of weakness. I still thought that showing emotions meant I was weak. I had yet to learn that showing emotions was not a sign of weakness, rather a sign that I am human and I am allowed to feel. I wanted them to see me strong and able to take care of them. We went home and went to sleep.

S.T.O.P: I ***STOPPED*** for a moment and reviewed the whole situation. I ***THOUGHT*** about it thoroughly and about possible consequences. I considered all the ***OPTIONS,*** then ***PROCEEDED*** to rapidly begin the process of separation and divorce.

Peace vs. Chaos: A Day in Court

We need clear strategies to resolve complicated issues.

Over the next few days, things moved quickly. Robbie was served the injunction order the same day. His brother Kumar flew in from New Jersey and was at the house. I updated him and advised him, subtly, to seek out the help of an attorney since the injunction hearing was on December 19. I would not have felt good if Robbie did not have proper legal representation. He was not allowed to come to our house until we saw the judge. It was a temporary injunction order, and we both had to present our cases. The judge would then decide if the situation warranted a permanent injunction. Robbie would get to speak his side at that point. I did not indicate at any point that I was filing for a divorce. This was of no concern to anyone.

Toward the end of the week, the clinic released Robbie to his brother. By then the tide was starting to change. I was happy to know Robbie was getting support. I knew he needed it. I was also prepared to be accused of causing the mess and to be told I was a terrible wife. Everyone needs someone to blame for his or her shortcomings. This was expected. If I were going to make this decision, I had to be willing and strong to withstand any backlash from anyone. I could not run anymore.

I clearly remembered what a much older person said to me once. "In life you get to make your decisions; if you fail to make those decisions, one will be made for you." I would make my own decision. It might or might not be the right one, but at least I would have made it based on what I knew. I would make my decisions with no intent to hurt another. I would stand up for my rights, even if doing so left me standing alone.

The days rolled on. I met several times with my attorney. He was also moving quickly with what needed to be done to serve Robbie the divorce summons. The injunction hearing was on December 19, 2007. I met with my attorney all afternoon and evening the day before to get the papers ready to serve to Robbie. The plan was to have him served when he arrived for the injunction hearing. By then Kumar had flown back to New Jersey, and Ramchand, his wife, his mother, and his sister flew in and were somewhere in Orlando. I was happy because when Robbie was served with the divorce papers, he would certainly need his family's support.

Robbie took advantage of my kindness; sadly, he mistook that kindness for weakness. He never thought I would go through with a divorce. He thought he could say anything, swear, leave anytime, come in anytime, not talk to any of us, get all his expenses paid, abuse me, and I would never leave. He knew I loved him, and he knew I would avoid divorce at all cost because I did not want the marriage to end. He knew how much the marriage meant to me. This would be one of the biggest mistakes of his life.

Finally, December 19 came. The hearing was scheduled for 10:00 a.m. at the Lake County, Florida, judicial center in downtown Tavares. I got up and tried to make the morning as normal as possible. Randy and Sam went off to school. I got dressed and went to the courthouse. My attorney called and said he was already at the courthouse waiting for a judge to sign the divorce order.

I went to the waiting area and sat down waiting for our case to be called. I was sitting alone. Robbie sat two rows behind me in the lobby with his family. His sister-in-law came up and gave me a hug. No one from my family was there, and no one knew where I was or what I had done. I was carrying a huge burden, but I should not have carried it alone. I now know I should have asked someone to accompany me. I will not hesitate to ask for help in the future.

We were all seated in the courtroom once our names were called. I was on the left, the plaintiff's side, shaking uncontrollably. I was extremely nervous. I had to sit on my hands to prevent them from shaking. Robbie and his family were on the right, the defendant's side. Suddenly, I saw a well-dressed woman come up and sit next to Robbie. I realized she was his attorney. My attorney was not there. I was afraid to move or breathe. What was I doing here? How had my life gotten so screwed up? What was happening? Where was my attorney?

Just then, I heard the courtroom door open behind me. The courtroom attendant, who was outside calling the cases, came in and tapped Robbie's attorney on her shoulder and beckoned her outside. His attorney walked out. Not thirty seconds later, she came back, tapped Robbie on his shoulder, and they walked out. It was happening. Robbie was about to get served with the divorce order. My attorney had finally found a judge to sign the order! Not two minutes later, Robbie walked back in with his attorney, paperwork in his hands. It was done. He was served. His family was leaning in to hear what his attorney had to say. I overheard his attorney saying, "We have to talk with her; she has filed for divorce. This was not what I expected."

I continued to shiver. I felt I was going to pass out. My attorney was still not in the courtroom. I started to pray. *God, please have him come in. I cannot go up there alone. I will die right here in this courtroom.* Then our case was called to the tables. No sign of my attorney. At this point, I was not sure what Robbie's attorney was thinking.

The judge asked us to stand and we were sworn in. We took our seats. I could not stop shaking. I was sure I was going to faint.

I did not hear the courtroom door open. It was quiet. I did not see my attorney enter either. I turned to the left, and there he was walking up to the table. The judge asked, "Who are you, may I ask?"

"I am Ms. Deowdhat's attorney," he replied.

"I was not informed Ms. Deowdhat has representation," said the judge.

"My apologies, Your Honor, but my client filed for dissolution of marriage, and Mr. Deowdhat was served. I am sorry I did not let you know," he answered.

Robbie's attorney stood up. "Your Honor, I was not aware either that Ms. Deowdhat had an attorney."

"Your Honor, I was not aware Mr. Deowdhat had an attorney," replied my attorney.

It was tense. You could hear a pin drop. I focused only on trying to stop shaking!

"May I see both counsels at my podium, please?" said the judge.

Both attorneys went up to see the judge. Whispered conversations transpired. Both attorneys walked back to their respective tables. The judge said, "Counsel, would you both step out of the courtroom please and discuss with each of your clients what they would like and then come back. Since this is going to be a dissolution of a marriage case, there are some things that will need to be agreed to by your clients."

Everyone went back to the lobby. Over the next hour or so, I remember little. There was a lot of negotiating. I agreed to allow Robbie to pick up the children in the driveway and to call me by phone to discuss drop off and pickup. The injunction was modified, but the divorce was happening. I did not plan to negotiate on it. Finally, our agreements were presented to the judge. The injunction was approved for one year ending December 19, 2008. The judge decided the case warranted an extension of the restraining order as a result of reviewing the case history and evidence. It would be in force until the divorce was completed. Things were moving quickly. By noon, we were all out of there.

I picked up Randy and Sam from school, took them home, and went to see my counselor. I did not go to work that day. The day finally ended. I was home with Randy and Sam. Robbie was somewhere with his family. That was of no concern to me any longer. I felt safe and an immense sense of relief.

I now know that since I did not tell family or close friends what was happening, they were not able to assist. I am now positive that family and close friends would be more than willing to help, but I have to let them know I need help. I did not have to go through it alone.

Facing the Truth: Alcoholism

Our problems are ours to fix, not someone else's responsibility.

December 19 was a Wednesday. Friday morning rolled around, and I received a phone call from Robbie's sister-in-law. At that point, I was getting more and more disgusted with the entire situation. Robbie was apparently luring his family into believing he'd done nothing and *it was a big misunderstanding.* This was one of his favorite statements. He gravely misunderstood me. Nevertheless, I listened to what she had to say.

She told me Robbie had been extremely agitated for a few days. This was not news to me. I had lived with this nonsense for twenty-one years. Finally, she revealed the reason she called. Robbie had made a "shocking" confession and he wanted to tell me himself. She requested I meet them for breakfast the next morning. I agreed. I would like to hear this myself. This would be news to me. Finally, I might get the answer to this madness. What could it be? I found it hard to concentrate at work that day. Finally, at last, Saturday morning came after a sleepless night.

By five thirty, I was on my way to meet them at a Waffle House. I pulled into the parking lot and sat in the car awhile. I really wanted to turn around and go home. What in the world was I doing? I'd made my decision. All this was pointless. It would not matter what he said. I'd had it with the fights, the cursing, the drinking, the abuse, and the disappearing. I was putting an end to the madness and getting back into my own life. Well, there was no time like the present to find out what *the confession* was.

I braced myself and walked bravely into the restaurant. There were very few patrons. It was a little before 6:00 a.m. on December 22, 2007. I sat across from Robbie. He was literally shaking—and he should have been, considering the situation we were all now in, I thought. I was angry and yet composed. I look back now and remember how difficult it was to sit there across from him and not reach across and choke him. Believe me, that thought had crossed my mind on many occasions, especially that morning. This time I really wanted to do it, but what good would it do? I sat quietly and ordered a coffee. I am learning I do not have to react to all my feelings, but it is OK to feel them.

Robbie's brother and his wife got up and went to another table. I was left alone with Robbie. He started to cry. He asked for my hand. It took all I had to give him my hand. I actually had to think about the request. We had spent twenty years together, shared two children, and the least I could do at that point was allow him to speak his mind

I reached over and gave him my hand. He took it gently, and I felt empathy for him. This was stunning to me. Because of the years of hurt, I'd become numb to any emotional feelings toward him, but I was sad to see him cry. I guess it is natural, as it is OK to be humane toward those in need or in pain. He started talking.

"I really have to tell you what happened. I am an alcoholic."

What? He is an alcoholic? That is the confession? I knew by then that he was an alcoholic, but I could not convince *him* that he was an alcoholic! *How about the verbal and emotional abuse? What is the cause for that? All the abuse happened because he drank?* No, it could not. I believed there was more to this than drinking and being an alcoholic. I was sure of it. At that time, I did not know much about alcoholism. I was ignorant of the effects of the disease and the symptoms that accompany it. Robbie continued.

"A few years ago I could not sleep when I started working nights. I would drink and fall asleep then get up and drink some more. After a while, I couldn't stop. I am drinking all the time now. Early in the morning, during the night, and all day," he admitted.

How had I missed this? I was sleeping in the same bed with this man, and I did not know he was getting up at night to drink! Was I that stupid? More baffling, Robbie knew what he was doing and did nothing to fix it! He continued to drink and drink more! How could a person do this to his family, his children, and worse yet to himself? OK so, it was the past few years, what happen to the prior years beginning with when you busted my head? I was still listening. Not a word was coming out of my mouth. I was speechless. Can alcohol cause this much turmoil in life?

"I am drinking vodka, not beer. I hid it in the barn and around the house so you would not see it. I can fix this. I am going to fix this once and for all. I have decided I am going with my family back to New Jersey to get help. I need your support to do this. I cannot do it alone."

What was he asking me to do? Help him fix a problem he created? My head was spinning. This had gone on for years, not to mention the verbal and emotional abuse, nothing said about that yet! I had pleaded with him to tell me what was going on before now. I wanted to help him then, not now. The years of emotional torture finally got to me. I was close to ending my life, losing my children and possibly my sanity. Now I was being asked to help? What could I do? I felt trapped. I wanted to run and not stop running.

Robbie was crying the entire time. He kept asking me repeatedly to help him. Finally, I started talking. God knows where these words came from, but they came.

"I am shocked to find out you have put us through this because you decided that alcohol was worth more than your family. I am very, very sorry for the situation that we are now in. However, I will not stop the divorce. I will continue with it. It is a long process. In exchange, I will support you 100 percent to fix your issues, but they are yours to fix. I cannot fix them for you. You will do what you need to do to fix them. I will pay for any treatment and wait for you to get it fixed. This I promise. However, I have asked you for years to tell me what was going on and to make a change, and you refused. I repeatedly begged you to stop abusing me. I do not want to take any chances in case you fail to fix the problem and stop drinking. The years of abuse finally got to me. I am sorry to say this, but it's true. Your drinking may or may not have caused you to abuse me, but you did abuse me. Neither you nor I can deny that. I am glad to see you have accepted that you are an alcoholic."

He was listening and making promises repeatedly that he would fix it. He was sure of it. This was his problem and had nothing to do with me. He told me I was the best wife a guy could ask for. He told me I was loving, caring, and giving. He told me he was sorry he made such a mess of things. He told me he would never ever take another drink again for the rest of his life. I believed him and felt in my heart that he would do whatever he needed to do to fix this.

I continued, "I will stand by you through all this, and when it's over and you are better, Randy, Sam, and I will wait for you. One request though: do not ever drink again as long as we are married and together, if we remain married. If you ever drink again, it will be over and I will not be this forgiving. Furthermore, besides the drinking, if you ever abuse me verbally or emotionally, I will not be this forgiving. More than your drinking problem, I will have no tolerance for any form of abuse." I was willing to give him another chance. I was not sure at the time if the abuse and the alcohol were related. I had a difficult time accepting that I was abused because of the disease of alcoholism. I agreed to help him, as I was probably not ready to walk away either. I needed more time to see if he would change. He deserved another chance, as this is the first time Robbie actually showed any signs of remorse. I did not want to proceed too quickly in ending the marriage if he was truly regretful. However, I was not willing to withdraw the divorce case just in the event he was not being truthful. He had lied in the past for a long time and I was able to base my future decisions only on the past.

I have learned a lot about alcoholism since then, and I am still learning. I struggle each day with separating the disease from the person. The disease or the person abused me, manipulated me, and took away precious years of my youth. It might be a while before I can truly say the disease was the cause. Today, I am not able to say that. I still believe blame lies with the person and not the disease.

After a while, Robbie's brother and his wife came back to the table. I thanked them and told them what Robbie had told me. Robbie told me he'd lied about the accident he had in September 2005 where he was rear-ended. He had pulled off to the side of the highway because he was drunk and wanted to vomit. When he pulled back on, he cut off an eighteen-wheeler that slammed into him and totaled his truck. There were two other accidents. The last one was in front of our driveway. He was ticketed. All those accidents cost us a lot in repairs and lost income. I had stopped counting how much money was going down the drain. Robbie was charging everything, using cash for God knows what. He spent more money on a monthly basis than the rest of us combined. I no longer cared about that. I wanted him to work on his issues and stop drinking and abusing for the rest of his life. That was the only thing I wanted. Not the money, not the house, not the luxuries of life; I simply wanted him to get better. I would spend whatever I needed to help him. I would pay for rehab and anything else. Money was no object. I explained all this to them before I left.

As quickly as I came in, I left the Waffle House. I meant every word I said. I would not stop the divorce. I would continue with the process, as it would take months. I would support Robbie, including paying his expenses to get better. I felt really good about myself that I was able to put my feelings of hurt and pain aside and do what I knew was the moral thing.

Throughout the process, I have learned a lot about alcoholism. I learned that alcoholism is a mental illness and a disease. It can be caused by a family history of drinking, drinking being viewed as an acceptable social behavior in a culture or community, or keeping company and drinking with others who are already drinking heavily. Alcoholism is a progressive disease, becoming worse over time, and can eventually be fatal.

Overuse of alcohol can cause both physical and psychological problems for the drinker. Physical signs can include withdrawal symptoms like 'the shakes' that can be observed visually when an alcoholic suddenly stops drinking. Other physical health problems can include liver disease, gastritis, anemia, and nervous disorders. There could also be psychological problems such as impairment in thinking, and changes in mood and behavior. These changes can sometimes lead to issues such as strained interpersonal relationships, marriage problems, child abuse, and domestic abuse. In many cases a person can begin to have issues with work or school, sometimes leading to costly legal and financial problems.

I learned that denial is a key part of the disease and becomes a major obstacle to recovery. Denial can cause a person to believe they have control over drinking and how much they can drink, this impairment in thinking can cause a person to deny having a drinking problem. The denial may not be intentional; to those who are outside of the disease, it could appear that the alcoholic simply does not want to make a change.

Alcoholism can be grouped in one of four stages. During the **first stage of alcoholism** drinking is no longer social, but becomes a means of emotional escape from problems that may exist. In this stage drinking is an attempt to escape from reality. Early in the disease, the drinker starts to depend on the mood-changing effects of drinking alcohol. He experiences a slow and gradual increase in tolerance of alcohol. This means that an increasing amount of alcohol is needed to 'feel the buzz.' It is common for drinkers in the first stage to start with one or two drinks before attending a social function and then increase social drinking to multiple drinks.

In the **second stage of alcoholism**, the urge to drink becomes more powerful. During this stage the drinker starts to drink earlier and earlier during the day. As her tolerance level increases, she drinks not because of tension or stress any longer, but because of dependence on alcohol. Friends and family members may begin to notice that the drinker is drinking excessively and having problems related to alcohol. During this stage the drinker may begin to feel more concerned and embarrassed about the drinking as well as failed attempts to stop drinking. Physical symptoms such as hangovers, blackouts, hand shaking and stomach problems increase in this stage. The drinker starts to externalize the cause of his problems, blaming other people and outside events for the drinking problem. The general sentiment is that "you've pushed me to drink."

The **third stage of alcoholism** causes the drinker to experience more loss of control that is noticeable by others. This means the drinker is unable to drink as initially intended. They may start out telling themselves that they will only take one or two drinks, but are unable to stop. The drinkers experience more serious personal problems including issues with employment, relationships, finances, and the law – all ultimately caused by drinking. In the third stage of alcoholism, it is common for the drinker to start avoiding friends and family and show a lack of interest in participating in activities that once were fun or important. Also during this stage 'eye-opener' drinks are taken whenever the problem drinker awakens. 'Eye-openers' may be taken to 'calm the nerves,' lessen effects of a hangover, or to quiet the feelings of regret. Problems of neglect starts to set in regarding necessities such as food, water, personal hygiene, shelter, and there is difficulty in personal interaction with others. During this stage, the drinker often makes attempts or promises to get professional medical assistance.

The **fourth and last stage of alcoholism** is defined by a continuous loss of control. In the earlier stages, the drinker may have been successful in keeping a job. Due to the fact that drinking during this stage frequently starts earlier in the day and continues throughout the day, few full-time jobs can be maintained under these conditions. In the earlier stages of the illness, the drinker had a choice whether he would take the first drink. After taking the first drink, the drinker typically lost all control and would then continue drinking. In the last stage of alcoholism, alcoholics no longer have a choice: they need to drink in order to function on a daily basis. In this stage of alcoholism, the alcoholic frequently gets helplessly drunk and may remain in this predicament for a number of days or weeks. The ultimate goal for the drinker is to experience the 'buzz' she once experienced. In the second or third stages of alcoholism the drinker's hands may have trembled slightly on mornings after getting drunk. In this stage, alcoholics get 'the shakes' whenever they refrain from drinking. 'The shakes' are an indication of a serious nervous disorder that affects the entire body.

Alcoholics in the fourth stage can be observed talking to themselves. When 'the shakes' are combined with hallucinations, the result is known as *delirium tremens*. This is a potentially deadly kind of alcoholism withdrawal that almost always takes place unless the alcoholic receives immediate treatment. It may come as no surprise that after an attack, many alcoholics promise to never drink again. Sadly, most of them do not fulfill their promises as they are helpless in this last stage. Consequently, they more than often return to drinking and the drinking patterns. Hence, the drinking problems continue to ruin their lives.

Fortunately, there are support groups today in most developed countries to help the alcoholics receive the kind of support needed to make an honest attempt to stop drinking. However, that help is underutilized by most alcoholics, especially those in my cultural community. An alcoholic has to willingly reach out for help and follow the guidance of those who are more qualified or those who walked the same path before, but were able to stop drinking. In the end, the alcoholic has to come out of denial first before being able to accept the help.

I learned I did not have the power to make an alcoholic stop drinking. Whether to drink or not is a personal choice.

As I continue to learn about the disease, I am also trying really hard to keep an open mind and not to blame the person or the disease. This can be very difficult at times, but I know my knowledge is in its infancy stages and it would be premature to blame either. However, I have resolved never to give power over my life to someone else.

Rehab

Be good to your body and it will support you in later years.

Lakhram came to offer support to us the week of Christmas. I was happy to see any family member. I was dying to tell someone how I felt, how I was hurting, how my life was turned upside down and out of control. I needed to let someone know I might have crossed the line into insanity, but I was sure I was not there any longer. I wanted to talk.

I talked nonstop from the airport all the way home. I kept on talking, and the more I talked the better I felt. I was talking and crying at the same time. I wasn't sure if I made much sense, but my brother listened. He knew I had to let it out. He is wise that way. I love him for all he is and for listening and not judging. Once home we spent the day talking and engaging the children as much as we could.

In the early afternoon, Robbie and the rest of his family showed up. They had asked to come over to talk to my brother. Robbie wanted to tell Lakhram himself that he promised to fix this and come back to his family. They spent all afternoon, all evening, and late into the night. I was not with them. I did not want to hear it again. Once was enough. The pain was too much, and the burden of taking care of the children, the home, and myself was a lot. I had no energy left to give to Robbie. He had sucked all of it away over the years.

Robbie spent hours telling my brother how he'd messed up. Finally, both sides of the family talked and agreed that Robbie was going back with them to voluntarily check into a rehab clinic. They would support him and so would we. Robbie did not want to tell Randy and Sam he was an alcoholic. He asked me to tell them, but I refused. He had to tell them himself. So he called them into the barn. I stood by him as he told them. The children were quiet as they listened.

The day ended after Robbie went and pulled out the bottles of vodka he was hiding. He took more clothes and shoes, said good-bye, and left. I promised to book his ticket and gave his brother a check for their expenses, a check they never cashed. They had reservations to fly to New Jersey on Monday, December 24, 2007.

On Sunday, Robbie asked to meet with me in private. I agreed. We met at my sister's house in Orlando, spent some quiet time, and then went to dinner at Olive Garden. I could count on one hand the number of times over the years Robbie went to dinner with me. Sad, but true. I should have been happy to finally go out with my then husband, but I was not. I went in support to someone who asked for my help.

Monday came, and they left for New Jersey. I was able to see them off for about thirty minutes. Robbie wanted to spend time with me. I figured he wanted to see how he could influence me. He was starting to see I was over his behavior and did not care anymore. He knew what he had put me through. He knew what he'd told me. He knew more than anyone, even me. I believe he had many secrets to live with. I was sad for him but trying hard to stay focused on myself. It was difficult to impossible at times, but I kept on trying.

The clinic he was admitted to, Endeavor House, is located in upstate New Jersey on the Hudson coastline. Robbie self-admitted, and I signed the paperwork taking financial responsibility. My health insurance was paying for most of it, so my cost was a fraction of the daily rate. It is a lockdown clinic with no outside contact for the first few weeks. The plan is to have alcoholics focus on themselves and nothing and no one else. If they are no longer in denial and honestly reach out for help, there are organizations and people to help. But, I was learning that no one can truly make an alcoholic accept the help. They have to accept help on their own.

I was really feeling the pain of separation for the first time in my life. I could not sleep at night. I was alone again. However, I kept myself busy. I was advised by my counselor to attend a twelve-step recovery program designed to help the families of alcoholics, so I started going to one such support group. The first few meetings, I felt it were a total imposition on my life and time. I was not the one who was drinking. Why should I be attending a support group? Nevertheless, I continued to go. I'd promised I would support Robbie. I would not fail. I would do my part. I would work, take care of myself, take care of the Randy and Sam, take care of the home, and go to the meetings.

I was going once a week on Wednesday nights. At first, I hated going and letting others know about my private life. I did not want to talk about me and what I was feeling. I felt they would judge me or worse yet view me as a weak and helpless person. Little did I know in the early weeks that the program would change the course of my entire life for years to come. I did not see it then, as I was still focused on the alcoholic. I was not able to focus on myself. As the wife of an alcoholic, I was never able to see me. Alcoholism is an all-consuming disease that affects each member of a family in different ways. I was on the front line of the abuse and determined not to move and have that abuse slowly and gradually get to my children as it had gotten me.

I kept in constant communication with the rehab clinic. Robbie's recovery was not going well. He refused to participate in any of the programs. He would not talk to anyone. The counselors told me they didn't believe Robbie really wanted to fix the issues. He was not ready, and chances were he was there to please me. What? They had to be wrong. I was sure of it. How could he not want to fix it? He'd promised! He'd lied!

After two weeks, I received a letter from Robbie. I was hoping the letter would say how sorry he was and that he was really working toward fixing his problems. On the contrary, he accused me of putting him there. It was my fault. What was wrong with this guy? Was he nuts? I was supporting him. His family went there every Saturday for family visits. All he had to do was follow the advice and work toward recovery. I was not happy about Robbie's lack of trying. He would not listen or do anything they told him to do. Well, he'd made a promise to me, and he would eventually learn that some promises should not be broken. If they are, then the consequences can be detrimental.

Robbie had run from taking responsibilities for his actions his entire life. The end of that road was now looming clearly ahead. I decided to see if he could fix this or if he was faking it. It would eventually come out. I was staying quiet. This was not mine to fix. I used to think that I could fix anything. I was now learning otherwise, thanks to my new support group.

I continued to see my counselor twice a week and went to the support group once a week. I was starting to understand what alcoholism was about.

I started to read a lot about it. I started to do research. I would listen to the stories told at the support group. I was now learning that alcoholism is a disease, like cancer, and a form of mental illness. I never knew that before. However, users can stop drinking, but only when they have reached their "rock bottom." No one and no event can force them to stop—not even those they love the most. Finally, I was starting to learn that the program I had hated to attend in the beginning was there to help me cope with alcoholism as a disease. I was starting to get the program one day at a time. I kept looking forward to the meetings.

I was still not talking about how I was feeling at the meetings. I was still talking about the alcoholic. As January 2008 ended, I developed a deeper understanding about how alcoholics behave. The symptoms are the same for every alcoholic. They want to blame someone else for their drinking. Robbie blamed me and I believed him. I used to blame myself. Not anymore. I finally started to talk at the meetings. I was now talking about how I was treated and how I was feeling. This was new to me. I never used to tell strangers, or even my family, how I felt. I was now telling strangers my deepest emotional state. I cried a lot once I started talking. I did not think I could cry that much! As soon as I opened my mouth, I would burst out crying. I would go when the meeting started and run out of there as soon as it was over. I did not want to talk to anyone outside of the meetings. I was still running away, but this time I was running from getting to know me.

I still find it hard to believe strangers in a support group I never knew existed would be the ones to hold my hand and take me on a path to recovery. I did not know how much help I needed until I started talking and listening to myself. I will continue to attend the support group indefinitely, whether an alcoholic is in my life or not and whether the alcoholic is still drinking or not. This program is for me, not for the alcoholic.

There is a big difference between talking the talk and walking the walk. Hold abusers to their promises of change, and if they cannot deliver then take action to protect and take care of yourself.

Face-off at Rehab

Laughter is food for the mind, body, and soul.

Early in February, I was scheduled to go meet with the counselors at the rehab clinic. It had been six weeks since Robbie was admitted, about the halfway mark into the treatment program. I made arrangements at work and took Sam with me to New Jersey. The meeting with the counselor was scheduled for Friday, February 1, at 10:00 a.m. I was hopeful. I felt Robbie was better. I felt it. My expectations were set high even though the counselors continued to tell me he was not working the program. I did not believe them. They were not telling me the truth.

I was excited to see Robbie. We'd exchanged a few letters and no phone calls. I was led to a small meeting room to wait for Robbie. After a few minutes, he came in with the lead counselor. Immediately he lost it. He started screaming at me and asked me to take him out of there! Me take him out? I reminded him gently that he had checked in to fix his problems and it was up to him whether he stayed or left. It was not up to me. This was not what he wanted to hear. He wanted me to make the decision to get him out. I did not intend to do that. This was not my problem to fix. I finally saw what the counselors were talking about. Robbie started swearing, yelling, and shoving at the counselor. I was scared and confused. I really felt he was going to hit me or, worse yet, hit the counselor. One of the most shocking experiences was to see Robbie becoming physical with the person who was supposed to be counseling him into recovery. He shoved the counselor a few times, slammed doors, and walked out of the clinic in below-freezing temperatures without a jacket onto the streets of upstate New Jersey!

I calmly got back in the car with his brother and his wife and we left. His brother was furious. After all the support and weeks of traveling two hours each trip to be there for him, it came down to this—not to mention the cost! His brother parked the car in haste and walked to where Robbie was on the side of the road. They had a few words. I guess his brother was pretty mad. He took Robbie back into the clinic, and we left, shocked and bewildered. It was not going well. I was disappointed. I knew now I'd expected too much and had set myself up for disappointment. By then I had learned little to nothing from my weeks in the support group. I needed to do a much better job of understanding the power of the program and applying it to myself. Boy, was I stubborn about change!

We were scheduled to attend the family session the next day, Saturday, at 8:00 a.m. Well, maybe tomorrow would be better. I was bringing Sam. Robbie would surely take one look at her and realize he had made a mistake. Sam, Robbie's two brothers, one of their wives, and I went into the meeting room and waited with the rest of the families. The lockdown clinic was a few blocks from where the group met. Not long afterward, a van arrived with Robbie and the others.

I could hardly believe what happened next. Robbie stormed into the room. The room was packed, standing room only. He began yelling, saying he needed to get the f— out of there and what the heck was I doing there. I was the cause of all this turmoil. He was focused only on me. His anger and hate were on me. He was staring directly at me. I felt if he had a chance, he would choke the life out of me right there and then.

For the first time in my life, I realized Robbie truly did not care about anyone, not even his only daughter. How could I have missed this all these years? Was I that naïve? No, I could not be. I was a professional with a master's degree and a competent CPA. No, I could not possibly be that stupid. However, I was definitely ignorant of the sly disease called alcoholism. I realized he could care for no one including himself. He was sick with a disease he did not even know he had; worse yet, he denied he had a disease.

I was seething with anger, frustration, and disappointment but did not move or say a word. Robbie did not even see Sam sitting there. She was extremely embarrassed, she later confessed. I am so sorry I allowed her to witness this madness.

He took awhile to calm down. I moved way across the room to sit. I was actually afraid. I was sure he was going to hit me. The meeting started, and we all had an opportunity to talk. Robbie was really trying to show some remorse. He kept saying he was sorry, crying at the same time. But it was too late. He had messed up once again.

The meeting was over; we said our good-byes and left. As soon as we got in the car, we started laughing hysterically. We needed it. Sam said we left her alone sitting next to a *madman* and she did not know what do to. We laughed and laughed. What else could we do? Cry? Not anymore. We knew everyone had done everything necessary and now it was up to Robbie. Sink or swim, he would decide for himself.

I spent the rest of the weekend with my family in New York, again not telling them why I was there. Sam and I flew back to Florida that Sunday evening. Life was back to normal as I knew normal back then.

My feelings of hurt, pain, and loneliness were starting to recede. I'd had high hopes and they were shattered. So what? I had to move on. I had the children, the counselor, and my support group. I would move forward little steps at a time. Eventually, I would be strong again. I might spend a long time being alone without a partner, but I would get used to it like anything else. My needs would wait and be put aside for now. God knew me and he knew my faith. He would take good care of me. All things happen in the order they are meant to happen. This is my belief.

Monday morning Randy and Sam were off to school and I was off to work. Around 9:00 a.m. I received a call from the rehab clinic. Robbie had self-discharged. He had decided he did not need them and signed all the necessary paperwork. He was released as AMA (against medical advice). I was not shocked. I had tried everything over the past years, to no avail. What made me think he would help himself if someone else asked him? I knew him better than anyone else. He had no issues lying, manipulating, and blaming others. What he did from here on out was up to him. The divorce was going through and the restraining order was still in place. He could not come back to the house. He would figure it out eventually.

That week was a blur with the family trying to get him to stay in New Jersey and trying to talk sense into him. Nothing worked. I was sure he was planning to come back home. There was no way it would happen. I was no longer the loving, caring wife who let everything go without saying how I felt. I was still quiet, but stronger. I was learning to live a newer and better way of life, thanks to my support group. I was keeping the focus on me. It was no longer about the alcoholic.

A week later I heard Robbie was coming back to Florida. I got him an apartment in Tavares, about fifteen minutes from where we lived. It was across from Randy's high school. I paid for it, had all utilities hooked up, cleaned it, furnished it, and ensured it was ready when he came. It set me back several thousand dollars, but as I said, I stopped counting. I was bleeding money by then. Between attorneys, the clinic, the travels, and the apartment, I kept spending and spending. But I'd made a promise, and if I had to spend the last cent I owned, I would. When I got out of this, I was never getting back in, and I was sure I would feel absolutely no guilt. I would ensure I did everything I could so he could never say I had not supported him.

I learned that people can show willingness to do things but for the wrong reasons. I believe change is a personal choice and no one can force change upon someone else. Change is also difficult, but sometimes it is a necessity, whether we want to change or not.

Back to Familiar Grounds

Change is just a word. The act of changing requires effort and discipline.

On February 6, 2008, Robbie's brother Kumar flew back to Florida with him. They came home and took what they needed to set up Robbie's apartment. Robbie was shocked to see I really did not want him back at the home. I firmly held my ground. I knew there was nothing I could do to get him to stop drinking. As far as I knew, he had not had a drink since he left back in December 2007. I believe he still was not drinking. I believe he was trying hard to hold it together. I truly believe he thought he could do it on his own. I learned later that alcoholics may not be able to stop drinking on their own, and if they can, it is very, very difficult. It is much easier with the help of a twelve-step program and support groups.

I kept doing anything to keep busy, working and taking care of myself, mind, body, and spirit. Robbie found the local twelve-step support groups and went every night. He had been told he should go to ninety meetings in ninety days and get a sponsor, who generally helps by keeping the alcoholic focused on recovery. Weeks went by, and Robbie never got a sponsor. He asked me to go to the group with him twice, and I did. He sat there and said nothing. He never spoke and clearly had no interest in being there. He was not there for himself; he was there because he thought it would make me happy. He was wrong.

Robbie asked me to help him find counselors, and I arranged for him to speak to two counselors. One was to address his severe anger issues, and one was to talk about what caused him to drink. He would show up late for appointments or not at all. He told them both he had no problems but was there because I'd told him to go. I had paid both counselors for several sessions in advance. I lost the money.

The days were going by quickly. I was still trying not to get involved with Robbie's recovery. I was going to counseling and to the support group once a week. Finally, Valentine's Day came around. Robbie had never done anything for this day either, much like the other holidays. On February 13, I came home from work and Robbie looked like he had been drinking. He was visiting the children. He could not look me in the eye, and he was a little restless and agitated. I felt like a thousand needles went through my body. I wanted to scream, but I forced myself to remain calm. I was getting used to being calm again, thanks to one of the slogans I learned in my support group: *"Let go and let God."* That simple slogan made my life manageable and it would probably be the reason for many of changes that came later.

The thought of Robbie drinking again made me cringe. But I had two beautiful children who needed me; I had to work, make money, feed them, and take care of them. Besides, I was spending all my time thinking of a forty-eight-year-old adult who should be taking care of us! This was wrong! I had to get out of this. I could not afford to think about Robbie's issues constantly. I had to make time for me. I knew a relapse could wreak havoc on my emotional state, and I did not have the strength anymore to fight the disease. The disease of alcoholism was stronger than I was.

I decided I was going to ask Robbie what was bothering him and if he had been drinking recently. He might not tell me, but I had the right to ask as much as he had the right not to say. I went to his apartment around nine thirty one night. He had been sleeping. I told him I wanted to talk, and he said he was tired. I asked what was bothering him, and he said nothing. I was very, very upset. I could not get the words out that I had planned. I kept pushing him to tell me if he was drinking or not. This was wrong. I knew better and should have not pushed or even gone there. He had the right to make his decisions; I should have left then or before I started to get angry. I should have practiced what I learned in my support group, *let go and let God.*

In the process of all this, I learned I had no control over Robbie's drinking. I knew this before I went there, so why did I go? I went because I was not ready to face a possible relapse. I knew if he relapsed, I could not face the emotional meltdown I might have. I was scared for myself. To this day, I strongly feel he had a relapse but did not want me to know.

He had to hide it as he hid everything else. I left his place crying. Robbie continued to go to his meetings and I continued with my support group. This was now our weekly life. He was going each night and I was going on Wednesday nights.

The next day, I discovered that Robbie had called his old drinking buddy. He had not told me they met up the week prior. I told him how disappointed and hurt I was and left it at that. He tried to make me feel better and was concerned that I was upset. I told him I was beyond upset; I was hurt. I could not understand how he could be serious about changing, but I was keeping a positive attitude. I was there to support him. If this recovery failed, it wouldn't be of my doing. This was one time in his life he was responsible for himself. No more would I allow him to hide behind my shadows or blame me.

On Friday, February 22, we went back to court to amend the injunction order to non-hostile contact only. The judge granted it. He told Robbie he was personally proud of him for making the effort to fix his life. This modification would allow him to come to the home with my consent only. He was to leave when asked. This way I had the right to tell him to leave if and when he started swearing, yelling, or screaming. This would happen if he was drinking. It was only a matter of time. I knew this process well by then. I was sure he was drinking again.

It was now early March. Robbie was still at the apartment. I had not heard or seen much of him for weeks. He would not answer his phone or return any calls. He did not come home to visit Randy and Sam as much either.

After a few weeks, he started to call me constantly asking to see me. Not Randy or Sam, but me! I hated it each time he called. He was not reaching out to the children at all. Our conversations would end up with him accusing me of being the reason he was in the mess. It was the same conversation each time. I was starting to get annoyed. Nevertheless, I was getting stronger and stronger with each passing day. I understood the disease better and had a lot of sympathy for Robbie. I hated to see how he was struggling. I hated it. I wished he were stronger to help himself, but the reality is he was not.

How could he blame his disease on me? How could I be the cause of another's drinking? At this point, I knew I was not the cause. I had not believed it before. I educated myself on the illness as best as I could and reached out for comfort from others more qualified than I was.

> *I learned the hard way that the last chance should be the last chance. I also should have known from my experiences that addicts or abusers will regret their actions temporarily, until the dust settles. Eventually, they revert back to old behaviors. I now know the last chances were for me, as I was not ready to make a separation.*

A Mother's Love

A mother's love never ceases for her offspring.

I would like to dedicate this section of my book to my former mother-in-law.

Around the end of February, Robbie's mom came to help and to spend some time with us. She spent over a month with us. I wanted to share with my readers my perspective of a mother's love for her son.

She really wanted Robbie to "fix" his life, and I think she would have done anything to make it happen. Sadly, I do not think she realized there was nothing she or anyone else could do. I had already tried to help foster change over two decades. I was sure that over the past few months, his family had had many opportunities to see how he behaved. I hated to see how Robbie was hurting his family. They truly cared for him and wanted him to get better. Robbie never listened to anyone and did nothing if he was not benefiting. He hated helping others out unless he was getting praises or a benefit. He would not willingly give to others. He was the polar opposite of me. Most of the time he would give because I forced him to do it, and after that I was sure he hated me for it. If there was drinking involved, of course he was willing to help.

A few weeks into his mother's visit, I noticed Robbie was very evasive. I started looking in his truck when I could. I had never gone through his wallet or truck before in my life. This was new for me. I knew I was invading another person's privacy, and I did not like how it felt. What was I looking for? I didn't know. I guess I was looking to see if he was drinking again. He wouldn't look anyone in the eye, and he kept on telling me that if I lifted the restraining order, he would be better. Fool that I was, I did that too, in late February. As I mentioned earlier, the amended order allowed him to come to the home at my request and leave at my request. I also advised my attorney to put the divorce case on hold! Later I regretted both of those decisions. Again, I allowed Robbie to lie and manipulate me. At that point, I would have done anything, hoping it would make a difference. I should have known better, but when you are in emotional pain, sensible decisions are rare.

Advice from those on the outside looking in comes easy, but when you are in the dilemma, nothing makes much sense. Simple decisions became burdensome. The fact I could get by one day was a blessing for me. To this day, I love watching the sun rise in the morning. I feel blessed to see it and say to myself that I have lived to see another day. I will never waste another minute of my life. I will enjoy every day of my life. This was my commitment as I was praying for help.

Not a week after his mother came, I believe Robbie was hanging out drinking with a drinking buddy. He was continuing to go the twelve-step support group, but what was he doing with his old drinking buddy? Why else would a person spend time with someone they used to get drunk with? I felt that if someone were serious about sobriety, hanging out with old drinking buddies demonstrated the opposite.

I felt I had to say something. I asked Robbie why he was out with that friend. His mom was standing there, listening to our conversation. He asked why I had gone through his truck and his wallet. It was where I'd found his buddy's contact number. I told him I knew he was drinking again, and since he was dishonest, I felt I needed to know the truth. I told him it was irrelevant what I found. The issue was the dishonesty. I reminded him it was his decision whether he drank or not, but it was my decision if I wanted to remain married to him.

His mom did not say much to him, but she was disappointed nevertheless. This was not her problem, nor was it mine. I am a mom and I know what it takes to have a child, hoping for the best. It must have been difficult to watch her son destroying his life, the life she nurtured for him as a child. I am sure she remembered all those times she took care of him. Unfortunately, none of us can fix this disease of alcoholism; it is entirely up to the alcoholic. It was becoming clearer to me Robbie did not want to attempt to try to stop drinking. I felt he did not want anyone to find out about it. I could not infer anything different from his behavior.

Toward the end of his mother's visit, I was tolerating Robbie a lot better than when she first came. I tried as hard as I could to remain calm and serene. I wanted his mom to feel good before she left. I didn't know whether Robbie would deteriorate slowly or quickly if he continued to drink. All I knew was I would not waste away with him, and I would not allow the disease to further affect Randy and Sam. We did not have to stop enjoying our lives simply because Robbie was an alcoholic.

I hope his family learned a lot and realized this was a disease that only Robbie could fix. I hope his mom knew how much I cared for her feelings. I also knew that if the marriage ended, so would my relationship with them. They are kind people, and I was happy to have them as my kids' grandparents and family. I would not try to influence their decision and feelings toward their son. He is their son, and they should love him unconditionally, the same way I love my children unconditionally.

I should have been more observant of situations surrounding my alcoholic abuser. For example, where he was and what he was doing. However, I was unable to "spy" into another person's life. I believe each of us has the right to some privacy. I do not have the power to make a person do the right thing.

Trying to Fake It

Hating another is hating oneself.

Around mid-March Robbie and I were starting to communicate better and his behavior was somewhat improving. I was not reading into it much, as I was expecting behaviors to continue to fluctuate. It is part of the disease.

I was starting to get out of the house again little by little with great encouragement from my longtime friends. Sam and I went to Lakeland to meet up with a few people. We had a great time; we ate, talked, laughed, chatted, and shopped. Sam got a pair of pants, three shirts, and I got some much-needed underwear! I simply forgot I had not bought underwear in years! We came back home around 6:00 p.m., and as soon as we got home Robbie began arguing. We were only in the driveway and not even in the house. What could I possibly have done? I simply asked him to leave. He did. He was spending a considerable amount of time at the house, but I would not allow him to stay when he would argue, yell, or swear. Robbie could go on for hours arguing.

As I lay in my bed that night, I realized I did not want to be in pain any longer. I wanted the truth, simply truth. How difficult could that be? I realized it was difficult for an alcoholic to be truthful. I was growing up emotionally. I was starting to let many things go that I had no control over. I was starting to curtail my sadness a lot, whatever little of it I had by then. I was detaching from Robbie slowly but surely. I was hoping one day it would be over and I would be completely detached.

The years had finally taken the love away. I knew by then it might never come back. I could not wait for the day to come when I would no longer think of Robbie and the pain he inflicted on me. God, I could not wait. He'd sucked the energy out of me during the most precious years of my youth.

On March 25, we had our first joint counseling session with a professional counselor. I arranged for the session. I listened to what Robbie had to say. I told the counselor I did not know where he was or what he was doing at all times. Robbie wanted to protect this well-guarded secret. What did he have to hide? I told her if Robbie did not learn how to stop drinking and stop being a verbal emotional abuser, the marriage would definitely end in a divorce.

We discussed going on a family vacation to see how we would get along, and Robbie clearly said he did not want to go to New York to see any of my family. Was this guy serious about getting better? The counselor wanted to know why he did not want to see them, and Robbie said it was a long drive. In the end, we agreed, with the counselor's help, to go on a road trip to New Jersey with the children. The only way Robbie agreed was if he did not have to go to see my family in New York. I agreed to go under those conditions. The drive from New Jersey to New York was probably under forty five minutes. Certainly not a long drive.

I caved for the sake of saving a failing marriage. At that session, we made three promises. First, I would not ask him to go to my family's house. Next, he was going to do the daily readings assigned to him by the counselor. Finally, he was never to mention anything from the past during the vacation.

Late March or early April, I instructed my attorney to put the divorce case on hold. We filed a motion to abate the dissolution of marriage case. I felt the pending divorce case could prevent Robbie from focusing on his recovery. I felt it was the right thing to do at the time.

We were planning to leave in early April. I wanted to drive for one reason only. No, not the cost; I wanted to see how Robbie would interact with us, being confined with those he claimed to love. If he really was into his family, this would be a healing trip for him. If he was faking it, this would be the most miserable trip of his life. I knew he hated to be with his family, namely me. This trip would show me his new or changed personalities where he made claims.

I had him move back into the house to see how he would interact with us as well. He relinquished his apartment the last week of March. Would it be different, or would he continue his bad habits soon after he moved back? I did not know, and the only way to find out was to have him move back. He moved back on March 28, 2008.

We left for New Jersey on March 29. Robbie was jumpy and wanted us to arrive. He was clearly uncomfortable with us. He demonstrated to me that this was the last place he wanted to be. He was forced to do it. I truly think to this day that he figured that if he went on vacation with us once, it gave him a clearance to move back to the house. He only wanted to move back, not change a thing. He would be pleasantly surprised. I had changed. He did not know this, but he would soon find out.

I learned that before making any commitment to a continued relationship, I must start testing the relationship. In this way, I can find out the strengths and weaknesses in the relationship, if any. I can then make an assessment and decide whether it is worth pursuing or not.

A Test of Change

Sometimes we allow ourselves to miss important events in our families' lives.

We arrived in New Jersey safe and tired. We spent the first day at Ramchand's house. We were sitting around the dining room table when the conversation came up as to how Robbie was doing with his recovery. I told them what he was and was not doing toward recovery. Robbie could not explain to them one thing he had changed. They were surprised to find he had not learned or improved much and was not seeing the counselors. The anger, the hate, the rage, and the disappearances were still there. We had a long discussion, and I told them not to feel responsible. This was between him and the disease, and the stronger of the two would survive. I felt he did not want to change because he either could not or did not feel the need to change. I told his family it was likely our marriage would end in a divorce.

Looking back, it's funny how I thought once he'd stopped drinking, his behavior would change. I was way off. His family was seeingsaw that he had not changed and they were in shock as to his behavior when they talked to him and asked questions. He completely avoided them at all costs. I was not surprised since I had seen this type of avoidance for most of our lives. Sadly, I was starting to believe the disease was stronger than Robbie.

I tried to remain calm and focused on what I needed to do for Randy, Sam, and myself. I did not cry as much as I used to. I was feeling better about myself, but sad for Robbie. I told his family about how he still blamed me for his disease. I told them about his continued relationship with his drinking buddy. I told them there were times he went missing and would not answer his phone. I told them I believed he was drinking again but did not have proof. Robbie did not deny it. I told them I was open to accepting certain things, but unconditionally I would not tolerate continued drinking.

I told them I was not about to give up another twenty-one seconds, much less years, to an abusive alcoholic! At times, I was starting to wonder if he really was an alcoholic or if he was using that as an excuse to justify his abuse.

After a few days in New Jersey, I took Randy and Sam and left for New York to spend time with my dear family. Randy and Sam were staying on behind for another week until school reopened after spring break. Robbie and I were driving back alone. This was a decision I made. I wanted to see how he would behave with me around. I had to know. If I chose to spend the rest of my life with this person, what would that life be like if there was no change? Would I continue in pain, disappointment, anger, and hate for the rest of my life? I had to know if this person was the one I wanted to grow old with. There had to be more to life than being sad all the time. What would I do when my children moved away if I stayed with Robbie?

Robbie told me on many occasions that he would never go anywhere with me, no matter what I did. He told me if that meant a divorce, that was what it would be. I never knew if he was serious or just threatening me because he knew what marriage meant to me. This person claimed he loved me and yet would do nothing to demonstrate partnership. I must have created the person he was today, unintentionally. I believed I loved too much and questioned nothing. I was trading everything I had to be loved. That was my mistake, one I planned never to make again. I never thought that loving someone too much would be a bad thing. In my case, it was.

Robbie and I left New Jersey for Florida on April 2. Neither of us spoke much, but a lot of relaxing and thinking was happening on my end. I made sure Robbie drove most of the way back. In the past, he never wanted to drive. He would never care if I was tired or wanted to rest. He would tell me to continue driving. All this needed to change. If he remained my husband, he would have to start doing his part.

When we were five minutes from home, Robbie went into a sudden rage about how much money had been spent on the lawyers. I expected this. He had to start an argument. That always allowed him to leave to go drinking. Yes, he would need to leave. Being confined with us for days was finally getting to him. He missed the alcohol.

He'd broken his promise not to bring up the past. I couldn't cry over nonsense anymore; life was too short, so I did not say anything and just let it go. I had been in this boat dozens of times in the past. I would no longer contribute to this madness. I was now able to keep my mouth shut and not respond. No matter what I said, it would not change the situation. By then I had learned the definition of insanity: *doing the same thing over and over again and expecting a different result.*

The rest of the week was uneventful. Robbie was back at the home now. You would think he would behave differently. No, that was not Robbie. He continued to be the person he was and behaved exactly the same. I was by myself a lot. I would go to the library or the park to get my head together and try as hard as I could not to get sad or depressed. I would listen to my favorite music and read as many books as I could. When I was by myself, I found a lot of peace. I tried hard to be alone. I worked late and left early for work to avoid Robbie. He hardly spoke to me and I hardly spoke to him.

As soon as I left for work, he left the house. No one knows where he went. At times, I thought maybe he was having an affair. All this crossed my mind. I did not want to think about it. I knew myself well enough that if I had ever found anything relating to an affair or infidelity, the marriage would certainly be over. Robbie knew I would not tolerate infidelity any more than I would tolerate physical abuse.

Randy and Sam came back from New York around the second week of April. I insisted we go to the airport together. This is what families usually do. This time, I would not let Robbie off the hook as in the past. I should have done these things much earlier in my marriage. I failed to see or accept that he was not doing anything for the marriage. He was married but acted as though he were single. He never even wore his wedding ring in all the years we were married! He drove to and from the airport, but he was clearly miserable.

On April 15, we had our second joint counseling session with one of his counselors. By then Robbie was back to his old self, angry, hateful, and lying. It had been three months since he was back in Florida and two weeks since he'd moved back into the house. I told both Robbie and the counselor I would not continue joint counseling sessions, as Robbie had issues he needed to resolve. Those issues had nothing to do with me. I would no longer attend counseling sessions, as I felt there was nothing more I could do to make him see that his behaviors needed to change. I felt really good about my decision when I walked out of the session. I did not talk about it again nor did I ask Robbie anything else about any counseling sessions from that point forward.

I was starting to sleep a lot better, regardless of Robbie's tumultuous life. I was letting go of a lot of sadness in my heart. I found I was able to stay focused on my children and myself more and more. I was not yelling at them anymore. I was not feeling as sad that my marriage would have to end. I was not feeling unsure about possibly spending the rest of my life without a partner. I was OK with all that. I was making resolutions that would define the remainder of my life.

I had some remorse. I felt the dedication and support I'd invested in the marriage was of no use. However, I understood the disease of alcoholism a lot better, though it was difficult to accept that the disease was the primary factor. As I stand on the outside of the disease a few years later, these questions still baffle me. I eventually started going to more than one support group a week. Furthermore, I forced myself to go to open twelve-step support groups for alcoholics in an attempt to understand the disease from those who are in recovery. I did not continue this, as I felt unable to keep an open mind about the disease. I was still not able to see the disease and the person separately. Also, I felt I was harboring some anger toward the disease. Someday I hope to get a better understanding and acceptance of the disease, but it is unlikely from my vantage point today. Only time will tell.

I have forgiven Robbie, but I was not able to forget many of the things that happened. I want to forget, believe me, I want to forget. I was told if I wrote it all down, then I would let it go. That has not worked well for me. I will continue to work toward forgetting the most painful things with the hope that I may forget someday. I hope that sharing this story will at least help with some of the pain and get it out of me finally. That is my wish and my hope.

I no longer blame myself for other people's misfortunes. I feel they are responsible for their own actions as I am responsible for mine. I take responsibility for my own mistakes.

The Final Breakup

To hesitate when the signs and directions are clear is risky.

On the morning of April 25, I woke up to get dressed for work. It was a Friday. I told Robbie I wanted to talk. It was now two weeks since he'd stopped talking to me. I asked why was trying so hard not to speak with me about his whereabouts and other basic communication that a wife had a right to know. I was willing to listen to anything he had to say. I wanted to keep an open mind. I told him I would not judge or get angry, even if he had to tell me he was drinking again. I wanted to know what was going on and how I could help.

Those words of encouragement had hardly left my lips before he became agitated. It was 7:00 a.m. and he was not drunk! He said if this marriage depended on him calling me or talking to me, then he did not want this marriage and I might as well go through with the divorce. He clearly said he would not change and did not care what I did. This was his decision and I could do nothing about it.

"Well, the way I see it, you are not giving me any choice other than to go through with the divorce," I said.

The conversation ended, and I went to work feeling like my head was going to explode. I could hardly believe Robbie wanted the divorce over making changes.

On Tuesday, four days after he told me he wanted the divorce, I had still not talked to my attorney. I wanted to see if he would change his mind and pursue his recovery further. Robbie was in the shower as I was working at my desk in my bedroom.

The bathroom door suddenly opened and out walked Robbie.

"When am I going to get a call from my f—ing lawyers so I can get the f— out of here?"

"You don't have to talk to the lawyer to get out if you want to. The door is open. There are four exits, pick one," I replied.

"Let me know if you called so that I can do what I have to do," he continued.

"No, I did not call my lawyer, but you can call yours if you want to. She can call mine and they can proceed," I answered.

He then said, "You don't f—ing get it, I am not changing. I want a f—ing divorce! I need to get out of here. I do not want this shit anymore!"

"OK, I understand you want the divorce. You don't have to keep reminding me," I said. "Let's call Ramchand and his wife first and let your side of the family know you have made your decision."

His brother and his wife really wanted to help Robbie make a change. They were supportive, and I simply thought that they should be the first ones to know we had made the decision to get the divorce.

"OK, let's call them. I will tell them myself," Robbie said.

It was as simple as that.

We spent the next forty-five minutes on the phone trying to convince Robbie this was not what he wanted. He insisted this was exactly what he'd wanted all along and he wanted it as quickly as possible. He was clear and concise. In the meantime, I was going through internal torture, thinking what would happen with his life and how he would throw it away. I was more concerned about him at this point than myself. What a shame, and what an ignorant ass!

The next day life-changing events began. I called my attorney at 9:00 a.m. sharp and gave notice to proceed with the divorce as soon as possible. I met with them at 5:00 p.m. and we spent the next three hours going through the final papers and settlement. They called his attorney and gave notice that he was to move from the residence by Friday May 2, 2008, at 6:00 p.m. and no later. He received legal notification, and he confirmed that he would move out without incident. If there were any incident, I fully planned to execute the restraining order. My mood was very sad. I had to make decisions I did not want to make.

I used to love this man at one point in my life. The madness had to end one day. Better sooner than later. There were too many wasted years.

Finally Friday evening came. I waited around at work until after 6:00 p.m. I had asked Randy to call me and let me know when his dad left.

He called around 6:15 and told me Robbie was gone. I drove home and prepared dinner.

I felt a sense of relief and concern at the same time. There was nothing I could do, absolutely nothing. Robbie wanted this and had made it clear he would not stop the drinking. He said he wanted his freedom, and Randy and Sam were older now and did not need him anymore. He said there was nothing more he could do for them and insisted he wanted out as soon as possible. His wish was about to be fulfilled. I was finally starting to get angry. The anger was the fuel that I needed to go through with this. The anger would cover the pain. Yes, anger was what I needed. At the snap of a finger, like that my life took another uncharted course. I was not sure where it would end up.

There was constant communication between my attorney and me, and finally a date of May 22, 2008, was set to sign the final divorce papers at Robbie's attorney's office in Tavares, Florida. We would meet at 3:00 p.m. The role of wife would end that date and time. I would simply be Mom.

In the weeks following Robbie's departure from the home, he frequently called Randy and Sam, almost every few minutes. He would call and say a couple of words and then hang up. I could see they were getting fed up. They got to where they did not want to answer the phone. It was clear to me he was possibly binge drinking. The night of May 8 he called Sam's phone after 1:00 a.m. and left a drunken, groggy message about coming and taking her to the bus. A few minutes later, he called my cell and hung up. I was getting angrier by the hour. I wanted to protect my children; if he wanted to toss his life away, so be it.

I called my attorney the next morning and informed him of the phone call abuse. We set the time limit when Robbie could call, not before 7:00 a.m. and not after 9:00 p.m. If he was using Randy and Sam to get to me, he would have to go to court to get to see them.

At 6:45 p.m. on May 9, 2008, I received a call from him. This was now a clear ten days since I'd spoken to him and since he moved out. He asked me to stop the divorce. I told him no, he had asked for this. The divorce was happening. Whatever happened after that was up to him. I was starting to get dizzy on this stupid merry-go-round. My heart ached for peace and happiness, and I did not want to waste my life. I wanted to cherish my life and to be happy. I wanted peace. I wanted not to have to worry. I wanted so many things, and only I could go out and get those things. No one would ever give them to me. Marriage to Robbie for all those years wore me out. I was carrying my load and his load. I was getting older and very, very tired. I wanted to rest. That was all I wanted, to rest for a while.

    I felt pain when I had to say no to his calls for help, but I had to stick it out. I had tried everything to help and nothing worked, absolutely nothing. I was not in control any longer of anyone's life but my own. This was a hard lesson to have learned. It took me years to get there. I no longer had any support to provide him, and I would no longer get involved with his issues. This change was one of the hardest changes I made as an adult, to stay out of Robbie's business.

I was hoping another would change for me, but I now know differently. To reiterate, change is a personal choice. I stand a better chance of finding peace and happiness by getting out of a situation that is not changing.

Negotiating the Divorce

We measure our actions against the background of our conscience.

I am not at liberty to reveal most of the divorce agreement at this point. However, I am able to talk about what transpired and what I was feeling toward the negotiation of the agreement.

Up until the day before the divorce, Robbie and I were able to maintain an amicable relationship and focus on the divorce settlement and the final agreement. We had many verbal agreements that we related to our attorneys. I wanted to get it over with as quickly as possible with minimal cost to either of us. During this time, I worked closely with my attorney to formulate the legal divorce document and what we wanted in the wording. We wanted the opportunity to write the terms of the agreement ourselves. My attorney allowed this and edited it to meet the legal requirements.

This was a process. It took about four drafts before we finally clearly listed what we wanted to say. I treated it without much emotion since I needed to stay focused on what was right and what I needed to do. I had to pay close attention to my conscience as well as the financial futures of Randy, Sam, and myself. This decision would affect us for the rest of our lives. This was about my children and me, and not so much about him. I would be the one left with the children and would be responsible for their expenses. I did not want to screw up their lives and fall short as a parent.

I continued to see my counselor and go my support group meetings to help me stay focused on myself. The feeling of sadness never went away. Whenever I thought back about when Robbie and I first met and how young, happy, and committed I was, it still brought tears to my eyes. So, I chose not to go back; instead, I wanted to use that energy wisely and go forward into the future and happy days that I knew lay ahead. They included Randy, Sam, and me. They included family, friends, and perhaps even a new partner. But they did not include Robbie.

How did I stay sane and focused? I kept myself busy and had great conversations with God. I worked overtime at home, went for long walks, and listened to great music. I went to dinner with Randy and Sam or to the mall, anywhere to keep busy. I could not go to the park or library, as that would have meant being alone. Alone was not a good idea. I tried to be in the company of others. It had been years since I invited anyone to the home, but that would not change for a while. I felt safe there and did not want anyone to come. I knew I would bring only those I truly trusted to my home, eventually.

I prayed a whole lot during that time. I kept my candles burning and asked God for strength. He gave me strength each day to get up, go for a walk, take care of the children, go to work, and come back home. It was a routine I felt I needed to keep, and I did. The mere thought of the next day or the past would put me into a tailspin. I could think only about what was here and now. I lived in the present. I thought of nothing else and no one else.

The weekend before the divorce, Sunday, May 18, 2008, I was starting to feel relaxed, and fleeting moments of happiness were starting to show up again. I wanted to ensure Robbie and I were both on the same page with regard to the divorce agreement. I had a draft copy I wanted to review with him. There had been many verbal agreements between us over the past few weeks. We communicated this to both attorneys, but I wanted to ensure we were both ready and there were no surprises the day of the actual divorce.

I invited Robbie for lunch. I asked Randy and Sam to stay in the house to allow us some private time. We were having lunch on the back porch. Robbie and I tried to stay civil toward each other. It was around 1:00 p.m. that beautiful May afternoon. I was in a decent mood but unaware that in minutes all that was about to change.

We started to eat. I took out the paper with the recap and wanted to go over the high-level version. Suddenly, Robbie's entire tone changed.

He said, "I have been thinking of this agreement of giving Randy and Sam each 25 percent and each of us taking 25 percent. I am going to talk to my attorney. I think we should split everything 60/40. I think that's more fair."

Negotiating the Divorce

We had talked about splitting everything four ways for weeks. This way the children would have some money set aside for their futures. I could not believe what I was hearing. I'd worked for almost 90 percent of what we had today. I'd worked almost one hundred hours per weeks during some periods of time. I'd even had a day and night job when things were tough in the early years. I'd spent years not sleeping because I wanted to work and knew as we got older we would benefit. Robbie never, ever had to work hard. He never knew how we saved the money, how I would cut corners to meet the expense loads. I'd sacrificed so much, and now we should split 60/40?

Never would I allow this to happen. We had already agreed he was not going to pay child support or alimony. I did not expect him to pay anything to help me out with the kids' futures. Most wives and mothers would not make this decision. This was against my lawyer's advice, but I knew it would be tough for Robbie to pay almost one thousand dollars a month child support if the State of Florida imposed those fees. In addition, I knew if I asked him to pay child support Randy and Sam would never see him again. He would live permanently in Guyana without a thought of his kids. He would certainly watch out for his welfare.

I tried to remain calm and replied, "Let me understand this clearly, the 60 percent for you and 40 percent for me?"

"No, 60 percent for you and 40 percent for me," Robbie replied.

"Robbie, I would have to sell everything to do that! The kids would be devastated. I promised them they would get to stay here. We would have been able to stay with the prior 25 percent agreement to each of us," I answered.

"This place is shit anyway. There is nothing here for them. They will be fine. I want to make sure I get what I deserve," Robbie continued.

What he deserved? He had used me, used the abundance of money I made, lived like a king, and never worried about how any of his bills got paid! What he deserved! I was getting extremely furious. I wanted to rip his eyeballs out with my bare hands at that point. I was not even asking for child support from this guy! Nevertheless, I forced myself to remain calm. I started to chant a prayer repeatedly to God.

"OK, Robbie, if this is what you want. Take a good look around because this will be the last time you ever set foot on this place again. I will surely sell all of it. We will end up owing the bank, so I hope you have your 40 percent of the losses to take to closing. I have my 60 percent. At the end of the day, we will walk away with absolutely nothing. I will sell it. I made all this equity in one lifetime and will do it again. This time I will be alone and without you. You bet your sorry ass I will give this place away for nothing! Now get out of my house!"

"To be honest, I don't think they deserve 25 percent each because they did not work for anything," he continued.

My heart shattered. I could not stand to look at him anymore. This time I was not able to control myself. How could someone be so heartless toward his own children? I will never understand this. I still do not understand it, even as I write this book.

"Get the f— of my house now. Just get out!" I yelled.

He had to leave immediately. I sat out on the back porch and started to cry. I could hear Randy and Sam in the house running around and laughing. They had no clue what took place. They did not know their dad felt they did not deserve anything. He was OK with them finding a new home and struggling. He was OK with all that. They had no clue. I sat there most of the afternoon by myself. I did not want to think anymore. I wanted it all to end. This was the one point in my life I regretted marrying Robbie and wasting away my years.

The days leading up to the day of the divorce were cold and dark. I never wanted to go through that experience again for the rest of my life. With no family around it was harder. I held it all in and stored it away to deal with those emotions later. For now, I had to do what I needed to do to get my life in a better place. I needed to be strong. I would have to cry later. However, I continued to go to my support group for some serenity.

I did not change the divorce agreement. I was prepared to go to battle. I promised Randy and Sam I was keeping the home and we would get to stay a few more years. I would keep that promise if it was the last sane thing I did. I simply said to myself that if Robbie did not agree to the terms on the day of the divorce, we would have to go to court and I would make sure that we spent every cent we had on both divorce attorneys. There would be nothing left for any of us. In the meantime, the money I made from that point on was not part of the agreement, and I would start saving from scratch. I would default on my mortgage in time. I would eventually be able to get a place to live with the children and the money to support them. I had no clue if Robbie had decided to contest the agreement.

I learned a hard lesson: divorce is just a piece of paper. It is by no means the end of a relationship or the end of my pain. I also know now that we have to take care of emotions as well. Unfortunately, there is no piece of paper that exists to take my pain away. The process of overcoming the emotions takes much longer.

Doomsday of Divorce

Faith is a demonstration of good things to come.

Finally, the big day came. May 22, 2008. This was exactly one month before our twenty-first wedding anniversary. I went to work and tried as best as I could to stay focused. It was hard to think straight. However, I knew the decisions I had made were the best a person could make given all options.

I left the office at 1:30 p.m. and went to the Wooton Tooten Park Tavares, where I stayed in my parked vehicle to try to clear my head. I was not scheduled to meet my attorney until 3:00 p.m. at Robbie's lawyer's office. I turned off the ignition and put the seat back. I looked in the mirror at my face; it was extremely dark with circles under my eyes. I looked like I'd run into a bus or come out of a really bad nightmare. I decided to lie back and take a short nap. I laid my head down and started to pray. I was very, very tired and getting sleepy. My stress level was probably at the highest at this point. I needed to shut down. I was asking God to give me the strength to handle that day. I had about forty-five minutes before I had to leave. I was getting more tired and was having a hard time staying awake. It was thirty minutes before countdown and I had to sleep. I could not stay awake. I was fighting it and did not want to miss the 3:00 p.m. appointment time. I do not remember going to sleep. The last thing I remember was asking God to take care of me and help me.

I suddenly felt like someone shook me and I woke. It was five minutes before the appointment. I had completely passed out for about twenty minutes. All of a sudden, the stress and the anxiety I had were gone! I felt refreshed and for some strange reason happy. I do not know what happened. I do not remember anything after closing my eyes and praying. What a feeling! There had to be some divine intervention. I could not feel this great all on my own. Someone helped me, and I knew it was God. He wanted to take my pain away and he did. I pulled the mirror down and was shocked at what stared back at me from the mirror. My goodness! My face was clear, lighter, even-toned, and very, very relaxed.

I started the car and drove confidently to Robbie's attorney's office across the street. It was now exactly 3:00 p.m. I was still trying to figure out what had happened during the twenty minutes I'd passed out.

I felt good and I was ready for this changing day in my life. I could handle anything thrown my way. My attorney came at 3:10 p.m. We both walked in to the waiting area and Robbie, his brother, and his sister-in-law were there as well. I no longer felt emotionally drained. I asked Robbie if he was doing OK, and he said yes, but I could see the turmoil in his face. I could not share it anymore. I was free of those feelings, and only thirty minutes earlier, I had been in the same mood as he was in, utmost confusion. God took care of me, and I would forever be grateful to Him for that.

Suddenly, without warning, Robbie went into a rage. We were all waiting in the common waiting area for the conference room to be ready.

"Who the f— is this, your boss?" he yelled.

"No, this is my attorney," I replied.

What I wanted to say was that he was the guy I was sleeping with! Robbie was pacing and wringing his hands. He looked like he was going to snap at any moment. Very gently, yet firmly, my attorney took my upper arm and told me to step outside with him. I was afraid of a physical confrontation. I was convinced that if we had not left the room, Robbie would have gone into a rage and attacked either my attorney or me. That moment, my fear of Robbie was at one of the highest points. We stood on the front porch, and this was where we spent the rest of the afternoon negotiating the divorce agreement. It was May in Florida with ninety-degree heat beating down on us combined by the afternoon sun. Both of us were sweating profusely under the layers of our clothing.

The next two hours were long. Robbie got mad, yelled, and cried. We negotiated, signed, sealed, and notarized the papers. At 5:10 p.m. I was out of there. It was done. I felt great. I simply wanted to go home to Randy and Sam. God had given me the strength when I needed it the most. He knew I was not able to get that strength on my own, so He gave me a helping hand. I needed to use that wisely and not waste it. I had not felt this good in years. This was truly a gift that I must cherish.

I went home and prepared a great dinner. I took a moment to reflect on some of the decisions I'd made regarding the divorce agreement. Robbie would not have to pay child support or alimony, and I would pay for and absorb all his outstanding debt, as well as pay him an amount of cash. He would have no obligations to his children or me monetarily. These decisions were clearly against my attorney's advice, but I wanted Robbie to have a good chance of making it in the event he decided to later improve his life or meet another partner. All I wanted was to be at peace and with my children. My new life was starting, and I wanted to start it the right way, with no resentment. I wanted to walk away with grace and dignity.

I was under the false impression that once I was legally divorced, all the pain would go away. Well, in reality emotions are not that black and white. A divorce did not mean the pain would end. It is a legal process, which is mutually exclusive from my emotions.

I asked God for help, and He helped. I have seen this demonstrated repeatedly in my life. I am by no means considering myself a great "devotee" of God, but I depend on God and I have said it clearly to Him. He has helped me in many ways.

Me and my Higher Power

God's power is beyond my definition and understanding.

I took Randy and Sam and went off to Cocoa Beach, Florida, for the weekend. It was Memorial Day weekend 2008. I used that time to get my connection back in full with God, He who gave me the strength to take each step, one moment at a time. I truly wanted to design the next phase of my life. I wanted to plan what my priorities would be from that point forward. I decided there were certain priorities in my life that I would focus on first.

To begin, I would start a consistent exercise routine to get my mental and physical health back to where it needed to be. I would reconnect with God by making it a daily routine to pray. I would continue to monitor my diet to ensure I was putting in my body only foods that were good for me. Next, I would stay close to Randy and Sam. I planned to continue having conversations with them regarding the disease of alcoholism. I would also continue to see my counselor and to attend my weekly support group meetings. I asked God to give me the strength to fulfill those promises. For now, this was all I could do with the energy I had. It was imperative to get my energy levels up in order to regain my happiness. I used to have an appreciation for life. One day at a time, it would all come back. I was finally starting to feel happiness returning, and it had only been a day since I was able to remove myself from the marriage and the disease.

The next day I started my morning routine. I loved watching the sunrise. I had forgotten how much I missed it. I woke up early and went out on the beach alone. It was warm, and the eastern sky was beginning to light up. The sound of the wind around me, the gentle lapping of the waves, and the occasional cries of the beach birds were music to my ears. My mind began to unwind and relax. My eyes slowly closed themselves, and I momentarily forgot the world. In those few moments, it seemed that I existed alone with God. My heart was engulfed in love, and I could feel the warm tears of love and affection rolling down my eyes. I began to address the Lord. I brought to mind any errors I had committed in life and asked for forgiveness.

Lord, you know them all and I ask for your forgiveness. I thank you for all that is good in my life. Lord, I realize now that I was so focused on my sadness that I forgot there was also good in my life. First, Randy and Sam are definitely a blessing from you. My family who loves me unconditionally and my friends who stood by me through all the rough times were also a blessing from you. I thank you, Lord, again and again.

As I opened my eyes, the world came back into existence and my senses began their normal functioning. The sun was climbing out of the sea, and what a beautiful vision it was. The divine light was the source of all life that enveloped me. It is no wonder that my ancestors as well as others in the world worshipped the sun as a form of God. Time stood still for me as I beheld Him and mentally gave my appreciation. I got up, walked to the water's edge, and stood there. That morning, it seemed as if God was everywhere. To this day, I still thank God for all the good in my life.

I went for a long walk on the beach. I must have walked several miles, lost in serenity and thoughts of happiness and contemplating the good things to come. I felt like a kid in a candy store where I could pick any candy I wanted, but there was such a large selection, it was difficult to decide. I was elated to embark on the next phase of my life with both children at my side. The idea of a new horizon seemed promising.

That weekend for the first time in a long time, I truly had a great time. Randy fished a lot, we ate out a lot, I read quite a bit, and Sam went in the pool quite a number of times. The weekend ended with a lot of hope for the future. I was not sure what lay ahead in the distant future, but I certainly knew what lay ahead in the near future. For now, that was all I needed. We came back Monday, May 26.

The weeks that followed were quiet and normal, with little to no communication between Robbie and us. I stayed out of his issues, and he kept butting into mine. I tried to talk little and did not communicate my actions to him or anyone else. There was no need. I kept going to my support group and to my counselor.

June 3, 2008, the divorce was granted. That same day I asked Robbie to meet me at the bank to complete the transfer of funds per the divorce judgment. We met at noon and I wire transferred the full judgment to this account. In addition, I transferred additional funds that were not part of the judgment. I felt I could give him more so that he could try to improve his life. I was totally detached from him and the money both. He took it and never said a word. I believe he was happy to have the money.

In the parking lot of the bank once the transfer was done, I shook his hand and wished him good luck. I also told him what he did not know was that I would have paid a million dollars more to get out of the sad marriage I was in, but I had to watch out for the welfare of my children, as he failed to do so. I meant every word of it. Sadly, my divorce caused me to take on additional debt of close to a quarter of a million dollars. I had to refinance my home to fund that debt. Nevertheless, each time I pay the mortgage I crack a smile. It was all worth it. Yes, the price I paid in search of my peace and happiness.

By now, none of my family knew of the divorce other than Devika, Lakhram, and Vic. I decided to plan a lunch at Puchie's house for June 8 in New York. I invited the rest of my brothers, sisters, nieces, and nephews I am close to. This was how I decided I wanted to tell them. I was comfortable with this decision and would not have the need to explain the story multiple times. I was ready to let the family know. I did not think much about their reactions.

I believe the thoughts I entertain continuously within my mind have the power to transform me within and change the outlook of my external environment. Good, loving, and caring thoughts bring out the beauty and divinity of the world within and without. I continue to experience this.

Divorce and Family

Your life is yours to live; live it well.

I arrived in New York with Sam midafternoon on June 7, 2008. We did our grocery shopping in preparation for lunch the next day. Finally, the morning of June 8 came. It was normal as normal could be. I was nervous, but I was also happy because finally after many years I could now tell the rest of my family. Lakhram and his family were there and so was my mom from Canada. Everyone started arriving around 1:00 p.m., and by three p.m. everyone I wanted there was present.

I asked for a moment of their attention as they gathered around. There were about twenty-five of us. I told everyone I had something to say and, up until that point, it had been confidential. However, after I said what I needed to say, it would no longer be confidential. I wanted them to hear it from me and no one else because I valued each of them. It was important to me they hear this from me first. I thanked them for coming.

"As of May twenty-second Robbie and I are officially divorced. It is final and we both agreed to this. It was a mutual decision. The reason primarily had to do with Robbie's drinking; he became an alcoholic."

I shared with them some minimal details. I was not ready to do a long explanation. It took about fifteen minutes. Most of them were surprised and shocked. There were questions thrown at me randomly, which I answered as best I could. I expected it, so I chose not to respond to comments if they were critical or involved a long answer. My family did not know the entire truth and it would take months to explain. It was safer and better for everyone to know as little as possible. Now they will know the whole truth. They will understand why I could not tell them the entire story during a lunch hour.

The rest of the day was quiet for me. I was at ease after I told my family. My mom started crying. At one point, my mom and I were alone. She had some questions, which I answered as best as I could. However, she told me my marriage ended because I traveled too much and that I went to school too much. I did not respond, as I knew her belief is still that a wife should not speak up for her rights but should be submissive. I was not abiding by cultural beliefs, and I expected my mother to say it was most likely my fault that the marriage ended. In my culture, a divorce is not taken well, and in almost all cases, it is the woman's fault. The expectation is that a woman should be more understanding of her husband's needs and stick it out, even if she is abused. Yes, that was my original intention, but I was not dealt that hand in the game of life. I had to play with the hand I was dealt. I folded and walked away with grace and dignity.

I enjoyed the rest of the vacation with Sam with my next destination in Toronto, Canada, to spend some quiet time. Sam and I flew home on June 15. We arrived home around 3:00 p.m. I had little conversation with Robbie or Randy during the time we were gone. I knew Robbie had been drinking the entire week because he called me several times swearing.

I went into the barn and the stench of stale beer almost knocked me off my feet. I had made it clear he was not to consume alcohol at the house when he visited or when Randy and Sam were in his care. I assumed the beer stench belonged to him. I was glad I'd gotten myself out of this miserable mess.

Robbie had asked to stay at the house until he was able to get a place to move out. He had given up his apartment back in March and had given up the room he was renting in Orlando. I told him I did not see any issues with that, as long as he stayed out of my way and paid an agreed amount for his stay until he was able to find a place of his own. In addition, I felt I needed to help him out as an obligation to the years of marriage and our two children. He moved into the spare guest room that evening.

I went to bed around 9:00 p.m. Suddenly, at 12:15 a.m. on June 16, there was a loud knock on my bedroom door. Robbie was drunk. He started yelling about my trip to New York and a bunch of controlling nonsense. This went on for about thirty minutes. Finally, I told him to stop it and not to swear in front of the children any longer. I told him if he did not stop, I would exercise the restraining order and have him removed from the home. He would not shut up! He was getting louder and louder. Randy and Sam were starting to wake up. I hated to have them witness this behavior again. He suddenly barged into my room. I was scared. This was just one day since he moved into the guest room.

I called 911 immediately. I was no longer apprehensive about protecting my children or myself. I told them I would like to exercise the order and have him leave the home immediately. They came and slapped handcuffs on him as he was saying I'd screwed him up for life. I was tired of hearing it! I wanted him out of my home. I wished then that the humane side of me did not exist. Nevertheless, it did and I could not throw him out the house until he had a place to live. I simply could not bring myself to do it. I was not ready to do it. I needed more time.

The officers read the restraining order and decided Robbie could not be taken to jail because the order said I had allowed him to stay, but he needed to leave when I asked him to. There was a technical language issue in the injunctions, which I was able to clear up the next day.

They took the cuffs off and told him to leave. He was drunk and could barely walk. He asked Randy to drive him somewhere. I told Randy to take him wherever he wanted to go, but not on the highway, and to call me and I would come pick my son up. They left, but I did not get a call, and when I came out later, I saw that Robbie's truck was still there, parked in the driveway. Both of them slept in the barn that night.

Randy was now growing up and at some point all this would hit him like a ton of bricks. I prayed and hoped all the training I had given him would kick in soon, or else he would be in serious trouble. I was not sure if Randy was able to handle his dad emotionally. I was praying hard for Randy and asking God to help him more than helping me. I wanted Randy to be a better man than his father was or ever would be.

The next morning I told Robbie to leave before noon and to take all his belongings. I went to work and called the local Howey Police and informed them to escort him off the property. When they came at 11:30 a.m., they called me back and told me he was gone. I could enjoy my home. How many times had I said it was the last time? God, I simply could not remember. I had given him so many chances, and he threw each one away. I believe now those chances were for me and not him. I needed time. I realize that now.

During the next week or so, Robbie called me repeatedly each day begging and pleading. I was starting to realize that the only thing that is consistent with an alcoholic is inconsistency. I had lived with that inconsistency for years. Now it was time to stop.

I decided to hear what he had to say, so I answered the phone. He told me he was going to New York and leaving for Guyana to live permanently.

"Well, thanks for letting me know and good luck and I wish you all the luck in the world," I said while nurturing the emotional pain I was feeling knowing my children would not see their dad for a long time if he left. Even worse, if he were to die while in Guyana, for any reason, I was not sure how the children would handle it.

Robbie asked if I would come to visit him, and I replied adamantly no. I meant it! He would surely beat the crap out of me there and dump my body in a canal somewhere if he got drunk enough. I was sure of that. I had absolutely no doubt about it!

I used to think others would welcome well-thought-out decisions, but in my experience I realize each of us is different and we deal with and handle situations differently. It is advantageous to focus and complete the tasks that are right in front of me based on my sense of value, urgency, and beliefs.

The Final Last Chance

Take care of yourself first, and then help others in need.

That week Robbie was really trying hard to make it work for himself. He was visiting the home a lot. He was still drinking but was more talkative. He really tried, but by then I was moving forward emotionally at a rapid pace. I simply could not take a chance hoping he would make permanent changes.

He was renting a room somewhere in Orlando again during this time. He was willing to talk with me and was willing to listen. For the first time in his life, he went walking with me without my even asking. We worked in the garden together. We were really bonding. I felt on the inside that he was truly reaching out for help, but I never lost sight of the fact I had walked this same road many times before.

He said he was sorry that he'd screwed up our lives. I solemnly reminded him that he'd screwed up his life, not ours. He wanted to know what he needed to do, and I simply told him to fix himself and all that he thought was wrong with him. I told him I had no interest in telling him what was wrong any longer. I reassured him it was his life and he would get to design it in a way that was right for him. He said he was going to New York and would go to all my family and try to make amends with them. He asked if I wanted to go with him and I said no. I kept on reminding him we were no longer husband and wife and he had no obligations to me.

I was not certain if I would give him one last chance even if he focused on his issues and tried to fix them. Not because I did not want to, but because I was not willing to take the risk again. I needed to give him encouragement, and I was starting to feel immense sadness for him.

Robbie left for New York the last week of June to see my family. I was enjoying the peace and quiet. I was starting to see how life would be without the constant nagging and unhappiness that surrounded him. I still thought about him a lot and about what he was doing. Was he thinking about the changes he had to make? Was he nervous about going to my family? What would he tell them? I tried to push those thoughts out of my head, with some level of success. I was looking forward to the long weekend to cook, relax, and complete my gardening projects. It was July 4, 2008, and the long weekend was coming up.

I was starting to think Robbie was braver than I'd given him credit for. I had been sure he was not going to follow through with going to make amends with my family, but I received a call from him saying he was at my sister's house. I knew he was nervous. I felt sorry for him.

Randy, Sam, and I relaxed and talked a lot that long weekend. We were enjoying the days. My life was falling into place without Robbie. I never thought this would be possible. I used to love him, yet I was ready and happy to leave him forever. What a different feeling. This was truly my detachment from love. I did not understand it before, but I do now. I did not have to worry about all those things I used to worry about: what he was thinking, would he get mad at the drop of a pin, would he drink and come home drunk. I simply did not think about those things anymore. I was thinking how I would enjoy the rest of my life, the children, and all the places I would go and things I would do. Going alone to places did not bother me anymore. I had accepted that I was done with the marriage and was settling into the single life. I hope those in my position will someday be able to feel the joy and happiness I was feeling right at that moment. It was truly the new beginning of the rest of my life.

I received a phone call around 4:00 p.m. on July 4 from Robbie. He sounded relaxed and happy. I was amazed, but then I realized he was probably drinking; and yes, the drinking was the solution to his problems and it did help him relax. On July 6, I received a phone call from him indicating he was returning home the next day. I picked him up at the airport. To this day, I do not know what he told my family during that trip. We met at the airport,

"How was your flight?" I asked,

"OK," he replied,

"You had a good trip?" I inquired.

"It was OK," he said.

He was cold as a dead, frozen fish. I did not expect this behavior, but later I guessed I knew why he was cold. I would call it "emotional manipulation." Was he expecting me to get personal and find out play-by-play what happened? Should I have displayed how grateful I was for him going to my family once in his life? I really did not plan to venture into his recovery any longer. I had worn out that path over the years. I drove home, and not a word more was spoken.

I must do what is necessary to ensure happiness for my life, and in this process, by all means, I forgive those who have caused me pain. This forgiveness is important for me to move on, as it removes anger and bitterness and brings peace and happiness to me.

The First Last Vacation

*The simple things in life can be the
most difficult to appreciate.*

The change process was apparently continuing. Robbie had decided to come to Fort Lauderdale with us for an eight-day vacation at our timeshare on the beach in mid-July. He had come only the first year for three days when Sam was two years old. That was the only vacation he ever took with us. I would not even call it a vacation. I was sure he was making an appearance because he thought if he came, I would see that one change and take him back.

I did not ask Robbie if he was going with us. I made plans like all other families assuming he was coming since he said he wanted to go. If he wanted to be a family like he was claiming, then he would finally learn that being family was a twenty-four/seven job. He would feel this for the first time in his life. I assured myself that after he spent eight days with his family, he would want to run away from them for the rest of his life! He would know this was not what he wanted. I was convinced he wanted to live a single life while having a family at the same time! This was a case of eating your cake and having it too. How does a person change behaviors, especially a lifetime of behaviors? Are behaviors changeable?

The week was normal for me. I focused on Randy and Sam as much as I could. I enjoyed my family members who were there as well. We were supposed to stay until Sunday, July 20, but we left a day early. Robbie wanted to go home, and guess what? We all wanted to go home. We had fun but we missed the dogs and home. Robbie asked to move back into the guest room, this one last time. I allowed him that chance again for him to try to find his strength to leave.

I was planning to do my part in this final and last chance. I planned to spend a lot of time with Robbie and help him in his process of change.

This he said he wanted. I was bent on not sabotaging his attempt whether it was a pretense on his part or not. That was none of my business. I had committed to providing the support and that was exactly what I intended to do. I would do my best.

Monday to Friday after the trip to Fort Lauderdale, Robbie did not speak with us. He pulled away. I guessed he was finally seeing what being a family meant, and he did not like it much. I clearly told him I was going to stay away from him until he got over his mood, and when he did, he could simply let me know. I had finally grown up and I would no longer give and give until I fell over and died of exhaustion. No, this round he would be the one to compromise; if he could not, too bad.

This was the last chance he asked for. I had given him many, many chances in the past, but this was truly his last. I ensured he understood it clearly. Whether he believed me or not, I do not know then nor do I know now.

One morning he said he was thinking of going to Orlando.

"Oh, I would love to go to Orlando," I responded. "Randy and Sam are still sleeping and I have nothing much to do. Let me clean half the house and I will go with you," I said. He hated to have me go with him anywhere. This would definitely have to change.

"Are you sure? I am just going to check out a tractor part at the store and will be right back," he replied. He was lying.

I was not falling for that line ever again! That was how the past twenty-one years had been. I kept remembering the definition of insanity. This time I was not going to believe him. I would go with him. Let's see how serious he was about being a better person.

"Yeah, I am sure I would love to spend the day with you," I continued.

I took the next hour or so and cleaned some more of the house. Finally, at 11:00 a.m. we left for Orlando. What a wasted day; we did not do a thing. We purchased groceries and came back home at 4:00 p.m. Robbie never had any plans to go to the tractor store. That was another excuse to get out to drink. During the entire trip, he hardly spoke. When I looked at him, his face showed this was the last place on earth he wanted to be. Words could never express my feelings at that point. Nevertheless, I accepted the situation for what it was. I could not change the situation, and I could never force someone to be a part of my life if the person did not willingly want to be there. This had to be a voluntary effort on the person's part. How was I not able to see this before?

Later that day I was mowing the driveway that led up to the road. Robbie pulled up beside me and said he was going up to Ace Hardware in Tavares. I said OK and thanked him for letting me know. I knew he was not going to Ace Hardware. Two hours later he came back home. He was drunk. He did not yell or behave as he normally did. I simply asked him if he was happy when he was drinking and why he had to lie to go drinking.

"I wanted to go to Orlando this morning and you had to come. I wanted to go and drink with the guys. I did not want you to go with me," he said.

Finally, he could tell the truth! What a relief! I never thought he would be able to tell the truth, to be quite honest.

"So you did not want me to come with you?" I asked.

"No," he said.

I told him then how I felt. I told him I knew he was unhappy and he complained all the time about not being able to go anywhere. That behavior caused the marriage to fail in conjunction with the abuse and alcohol. I told him I was OK with all that and was moving ahead knowing that I did everything I could have possibly done. In the end, he'd made the choice not to change.

There is a saying that goes, "Be careful what you wish for because one day God will grant you that wish." Time would tell when God would grant Robbie his wish, the wish to be alone. I hoped he would appreciate it and enjoy what he wanted, the freedom to go and be anywhere without anyone asking him or questioning him. I prayed for him that he would enjoy that freedom. It was all up to him now.

It was a quiet night. We were both sitting on the swing on the patio. I simply told him not to change his life for me. It was not worth it. I told him he would be unhappy in the long run and would blame me for his unhappiness. I said I knew he did not love me and it hurt because I had truly loved him. He would never be happy with me because I would not put up with his lies, manipulation, and control again for a single day. I told him I was a good wife and a good person; I knew it now, though I had doubted it in the past. I deserved someone who would want to be with me and love me unconditionally. If that person never crossed my path, I was OK with it. Life for me had to be better than it was now. I told him he'd worked hard to have the freedom, so he should enjoy it and not screw it up. I wanted to be free to move on with my life and be happy. I wanted him to leave me in peace. I told him when a person truly loved someone, he or she would put the other person's happiness ahead of his or her own. Robbie was never able to do that for me or his children. I did not blame him in any way.

He and I both knew that was the ultimate truth. How we ended up there, I had no clue, but here we were. He listened because sadly, it was true.

I believe in Robbie's mind he was never married. He was never committed to anyone. He was never called to the mat until a few years ago, and the marriage ended because I told him to step up. This relationship would have never survived, and we were never meant

to grow old together. I finally grew up and I now know what love really means.

Love is one of the things we give freely, unselfishly, and unconditionally. I believe most of us hold on to it and chose not to give it fully for a variety of reasons. All other emotions I had such as hate, anger, and remorse had left my heart. The love was about to go, but I tried as hard as I could to hang on to that and keep it alive. I promised myself that if I lost my love for others, then I would have truly lost myself. I planned never to lose me ever again. I promised myself I would try really, really hard. I wanted my children to believe in love and not lose faith in it. I would leave it up to God now. I let go of all else except love. God was in charge, and he would help me preserve the one thing I believed in the most, love.

I remember the scriptures of my religion saying that God is the seed from which the universe sprouted. I am a plant that came from that seed; therefore, I have inherited many qualities of the host plant. My God loves. I will love.

The Last Failed Control

We are only in control of our actions and ourselves.

It was August 7, 2008, and that night I planned to go to my normal weekly support group. This was the only hour I had to spare to take care of me. I looked forward to Thursday for the opportunity to focus on me and work on my issues. I had learned a lot about myself over the year and a half since I had been going. I'd learned to spend a lot more time focusing on me and my state of mind and my affairs. It was hard at first, but little by little, Robbie was coming out of my head. Those times when I did not think of him were blessings for me. This would allow me time to think of the children and me. It was a completely new way of thinking.

When I came home from work, Robbie was there watching TV. He had a scary look on this face, somewhat the same as the look the night he'd said he was going to get the gun to end it all. That told me not to say a word and to keep very, very quiet. I asked Randy and Sam to be quiet as well. I had not seen this look in months. I started to prepare dinner. It was about 6:20 p.m. I had lots of time before my support group, which started at 8:00 p.m.

Out of nowhere, Robbie said, "Are you going to that f—f—ing group again?"

Both children scampered off to their rooms. How sad. They knew when he started talking, it was going to be trouble. I promised myself that I would not get into arguments with him or the disease.

"Why yes, and I am looking forward to going," I said calmly.

"Well, I am going with you today to see what the f— they do there."

"You could save yourself the trip. We focus on how to make ourselves and our lives better and happier. If you are interested in that, I am in full support of you going. You don't have to go to the one I am going to. You could go to another one if you want to," I replied.

"Well, I am going to go to that one and ask them why they have to take f—ing two hours every week," he said.

He went on and on about my support group. He blamed it for causing our marriage to fail. He blamed my family again and again. By now, I'd learned the only thing that was consistent with Robbie was his swearing and blaming and his inconsistent behavior. He was drunk and had that glazed look in his eyes, the dangerous look, the look to stay away from.

I was glad I was recovering and moving on, becoming stronger. This was not bothering me as much as it had in the past, as I was still learning that his behaviors were primarily related to the disease of alcoholism.

He started to get dressed around 7:00 p.m. He was urging me the entire time.

"Hurry up!" he said.

"I normally leave around seven forty-five, but if you want to go ahead, be my guest. I will see you there," I said.

"What, you don't want to go with me?" he asked.

"Please, you are not going with me; no one goes with anyone. Each of us goes by ourselves to focus on ourselves. We talk about ourselves and what we can do to better our own lives," I answered.

"Well I hope you are not going to f—ing talk about me there,"

"That never happens because when I am there I usually do not think about anyone else, including you. I think about myself and how alcoholism has affected my life."

My tone was calm and without anger. I was proud of myself that I was able to remain relaxed and truly not be bothered. I had learned a lot in the past year or so.

My relaxed behavior was really starting to bother him. I began talking randomly to kill the time. I told him I knew he was trying to control and manipulate me into not going, but that was not working anymore. My life belonged to me, and if he wanted to control a life, it would be great if he would start with his own.

I knew he had drunk a lot that day, so any discussion with him was pointless. It was sad, but there was nothing I could do except watch him destroy his life one day at a time, one drink at a time.

I finished cooking, got dressed, and went to my car. Robbie came out and got in my car before I could drive off. He was dressed in dark sunglasses, a knit winter hat, a London Fog insulated winter jacket, blue latex gloves, a black T-shirt, corduroy black pants, and black shoes. Can you imagine the look? It was August in Florida! It was literally over ninety-five degrees with the humidity equally high. He was dressed to go skiing. By the way, he'd asked Sam how he looked.

"Ugly," Sam had said without looking at him. She was probably embarrassed. He asked Randy as well.

"You look normal," Randy replied. I wanted to burst out laughing. I don't think Randy really cared.

Robbie was doing this, thinking I would get embarrassed and not go to the meeting. He would have to learn the hard way. He was swearing and arguing the entire drive. I simply drove and was at peace. It was a good test for me to see if he was able to grab my serenity. He was not.

When we arrived, it was almost dark.

"Don't introduce me to anyone. I can't stand those f—ing no-good piece-of-shit people," he said.

"Once I walk in that door I do not care what you say or do. I am here to focus on me and me alone," I said.

"I will sit next to you," he replied.

"You can sit where you please. There are lots of chairs around," I advised.

I found a chair and he found one. There were no chairs next to me, so Robbie had to sit away from me out of talking range. I loved it. He got up at least three times and walked out of the room, came back, and walked out again. He was restless. He was on his own. I was not embarrassed, not unhappy, but sad for him.

I wanted to tell him, "I am sorry, Robbie. It was your life and you got to do what you wanted with it. You wanted freedom and not to be responsible for anyone; you now have that chance. Only time will tell what you will do with it." But it would not have mattered.

The chairperson must have figured out who he was: me, an Indian woman, and Robbie, an Indian man who kept staring at me. She said to him, "Are you a newcomer with us?"

"I am here because she asked me to come," Robbie responded.

"That's OK; however you came does not matter as long as you are here. You are in the right place. Thanks for joining us today. What is your name?" she asked.

"Robbie," he answered.

"OK, Robbie, welcome to our Thursday night support group," she said nicely.

Robbie was extremely uncomfortable. I knew he was sorry he'd come. I knew his intent was to sabotage my recovery. He'd had so much help he had thrown out the window, and he refused to listen to anyone.

Robbie got up and left fifteen minutes into the hour. He never came back in.

I went to my car once the meeting was over. He was there waiting. I drove to the grocery store with him swearing and complaining. I had my serenity and no one was taking that away. I had worked hard for it. It was mine to keep.

I ignored him. I purchased some groceries and walked back out to my car. He was standing at the passenger side door, and the car was locked. I had the keys. I opened the trunk and put the groceries in. I walked to the driver side and opened my door. I did not use the remote in case it opened all the doors. I wanted only my door to open. I got in, started the car, shifted into reverse, and started to back away with him standing outside the locked passenger side door. We were almost ten miles from home.

"Wait, wait," he said.

I rolled down his side window about one inch and said slowly, "I am only going to say this once. You get in and shut up and I will take you to your truck at home. If you say one word between here and home, I will stop the car and ask you to get out, and if you do not I will have you removed from my car by calling law enforcement. I no longer want to listen to your swearing, hate, and angry outbursts. When I get home, I am going to have dinner, take a shower, and go to bed. I expect you to be gone or out of my sight by the time I come out of the shower. I am only to going to open the car door if you agree to this. Tell me now or walk home."

"I will not say anything," he quickly agreed. I opened the door, he got in, and I drove home. Not one word was spoken by anyone. I did what I said I was going to do. I showered and went to bed and slept soundly.

I felt generally good about how I'd handled the situation and stood my ground. The only thing Robbie said when we got home was, "I am going to get out of here when the time is right and when I am ready." I walked away.

Why couldn't people live peacefully without hurting others? I will forever try to be careful and not hurt others the way I was hurt. This is a promise to myself. I will rise above difficult situations and deal with my feelings without lashing out at others. Hopefully, someday I will meet another person who will share these goals, and if there is no one out there, then I guess I will spend the remaining years of my life alone. It will be fine. I know my decisions had consequences. I plan to fully face my consequences, whatever they are.

I already knew Robbie would leave because he could not make sacrifices for his family—and since he was not getting everything done his way anymore, why stick around? He would not last long in this situation with me or anyone else unless he decided to make a change. He would leave once he realized he was not able to get me to give into his control and manipulating ways. He had lost his victim, me.

I told him he was free to go and I would not hold him accountable for anything or blame him for anything. I would blame the disease of alcoholism. I told him I was ready and he should feel free to leave when he wanted to leave. Life with me would never be the same and he would never be happy because for once in his life he had to think about someone other than himself. I told him love had nothing to do with it. Anger, control, abuse, and alcohol had everything to do with it. Love alone could not save this marriage.

When we love another person, we have to know how to let things go and how to compromise. Robbie never had to do anything much in the entire twenty-one years of marriage. I did it for him and me both. This was a big mistake. If I had known what I knew now from the beginning, then maybe there would have been a chance of saving this marriage.

I was starting to get sad again, as I saw the final and last end approaching. My emotions about the final separation were stabilizing; however, I was feeling sadness for Robbie. I knew he was not prepared. He was still drinking a lot and had stopped talking to everyone about his disease.

I was looking at things in my life I needed to change or improve, and then doing what I needed to do to make positive changes. Sometimes it was difficult, but I gave it my best shot. Giving up this marriage was difficult, yet I knew it was the right thing to do and I was ready for that final walk.

I used to be a happy person who loved to laugh, make others laugh, and be happy. How could I stay in this marriage without eventually losing my core? I had to make this sacrifice for me. I had to take care of me. I wanted to share my life with someone, but that someone had lost his way a long time ago. For whatever reason, I was too blind to see it earlier.

In bed that night, I stayed awake for some time and started to think. Everything was starting to make sense. Robbie had allowed the divorce to go through because he knew he could not stop drinking. He also knew once I figured out that he had no intentions of stopping, he would have to leave. He'd made sure he got the money. Yet he still wanted to try to see if he was able to exert control over me. I guess each of us watches out for ourselves at some time or another in life. I would watch out for my children and me. This was my priority for today.

I no longer fall for the line "I love you." I think it is an overused line, and many of us have no clue as to the huge responsibilities attached to it. I think it is only magical when we embrace the obligations associated with it. I have said this on many occasions: love is so simple, but the responsibilities of loving someone are insurmountable.

The Last Confrontation

Bottling up feelings may not be a good thing. We should express them in a safe and healthy way.

On Sunday, August 24, 2008, I got up, fixed breakfast for everyone, and started cleaning the house and doing my chores. Robbie sat on the sofa all day and did not move. He looked really mad. He looked at me with such hate in his eyes, I cringed on the inside. What did I ever do to him? I had no idea, except standing up for myself. I was starting to wonder when he would find a place of his own and move out. It had now been a few weeks.

I finished around 2:00 p.m. Then I sat in the chair next to him.

"Robbie, if you want to go out somewhere, it's OK; you can go. I'm not mad anymore. We are no longer married. There is no obligation to me. I hate to see you so sad to be here, as if you are in a prison. You are out all day Monday to Friday and so happy. When it's the weekend or time with the kids on evenings and weekends, you are so sad and look so mad. Please try to find a place and live your life the way you want to live it," I said.

"I will have to go out later," he said.

"OK, but I don't need to know. You can go where you want and not tell me. I don't care to know. I am no longer your wife. You must try and remember that," I said.

I started fixing dinner around 4:00 p.m. It was eerily quiet. Robbie came into the kitchen to help me.

"You know, Robbie, this is all it takes to make a relationship work. Two people helping each other. In time, you may find another to share your life. I hope you learned from this failed marriage. These are the little changes, asking if I need help once in a while. You never asked me before in all those years we were together. Too bad it came after it's all over," I said.

He turned and looked at me squarely in the eyes and said without any sign of remorse or hesitation, "Does anyone ever change? I am not changing and never planned to from the beginning."

I did not react. I was not surprised. He'd wanted out for a long time and he'd led us along for a very bumpy ride. Why? Only he could answer that question, as I still have no clue.

"OK, thanks for letting me know," I said.

I went outside. I needed to get out of the house. Robbie came outside looking furious. He was in a tremendous turmoil, as I could see from the expression on his face. I could see every line on his forehead. I walked up to him.

"You know, Robbie, you don't have to be mad. If this was your decision, I am OK with it. It does not matter how I feel about it, as long as you are happy with your decision."

I did not know what else to say. I tried not to think about the right things to say to him, but I couldn't think of anything else. It felt as if I were drowning quickly and speaking in circles. Around 6:00 p.m. he took off. He said he was going to look for a job he'd seen. I knew he went to drink. It was a Sunday.

I proceeded to finish dinner. We were sitting outside when Robbie came back after about two hours or so. Randy and Sam were playing with the dogs, and I was trying to look normal. I asked him how it went looking for that job, to make casual conversation. He looked drunk or high.

"It's f—ing Sunday, who the hell would be there?" he answered.

He was upset because he knew he had been drinking and was lying. I told him I was sorry to hear that. I was still sitting on the swing, and the children were still playing around with the dogs. Robbie went in the house and suddenly came out again. He seemed agitated.

"Those f—ing people in Jersey City, I told those motherf—ers that I wanted to go to Guyana from the beginning and that I did not want this shit anymore, wife and kids. I did not want wife and kids. All I wanted was them to book my ticket for me to leave from the start," he said.

"Who are you talking about, and who stopped you from going?" I asked.

"Mom and Dad and the rest of those pricks," he answered.

I was starting to boil over. Finally, he was telling the truth. This was how he told the truth. He had to swear before he told a truth. The lies were so easy to tell, but the truth was hard. He was sure he wanted to go to Guyana, but he did not have the balls to leave. He had to make sure he made my life and the lives of the children miserable in the process. He did not want to be blamed for the marriage ending, but he was quite prepared for me to be blamed and abused. He was hoping for me take the fall for him. This time he would finally hear me out!

I started yelling. I was mad and I lost it. I had never in my life yelled that much at anyone. I was shaking uncontrollably. I had to get it out of me. I had to. It was all bottled up inside. I exploded.

"You f—ing son of a bitch, your eighty-year-old father is on his deathbed and far be it from you to offer him some help. You f—ing sit here and blame him and your poor mother who was supposed to book your f—ing ticket to go to Guyana. What the f— is wrong with your f—ing mouth or hand? You want to go to Guyana, go, f—ing book your own ticket! You need someone to wipe your sorry ass again? Go to the piece-of-shit drinking buddies you hang with and get them to f—ing book your ticket. You want someone to spoon-feed you and you had me to do that; now you want your old parents to take the blame for your f—ing problems. You are a fifty-year-old man and it's time you f—ing make some decisions for yourself. No one owes you anything, especially them. You have no shame. As for my family, they had nothing to do with your f—ing problems. You have the nerve to sit here swearing and blaming both my and your families when you are the only one to be blamed for your own f—ing problems. You knew from day one you did not plan to make a change and you planned all along to leave, but you did not have the balls to take the responsibility for it. You wanted me to be blamed.

"Well, guess what, I do not give two shits whose fault it is, just leave. I want you to get the f— out of here Friday by 2:00 p.m. I want to take care of my kids for the long weekend, and I do not want your f—ing ass to make it miserable. You are one miserable son of a bitch and you want everyone to feel bad for you. Your lies finally wrapped your ass up, and it's caught up with you. You told so many lies, you can't see the forest for the trees. You yourself don't know what the truth is. Just get the f— out of here Friday and take every f—ing thing with you. Anything you leave will get thrown out or sold. I don't give a f— anymore. Get all your stuff from the house, and if you even look at me, it will be the last second you spend here. Stay the f— out of my way and I will stay the f— out of yours. Your prayers have been answered; finally you get to go and enjoy the freedom that the kids and I paid for. Yes, that I paid for with my money! Get out of my life. Your relationship with your kids is up to you. You will never, ever have me again for the rest of your sorry-ass life. That may be the best thing ever for you!" I screamed at the top of my lungs.

I felt like dying and my head was bursting open. I could not remember the last time I was this mad or if I had ever been that mad. Randy and Sam were in the house, and I was sure they heard some of it. It was sad. I could not afford to put them through this again. In the past, I had lost my voice to stand up, but not now. I was drained of all energy. How I made it into the house, I have no recollection.

I went to bed and fell asleep. My body was going down and I could not bring it back up. I was very, very limp. I had no energy left in my body. This had to change, for the last time.

I learned that standing up for myself took a lot of energy and effort. I also learned that when I bottled up feelings for a long time, there came a time when I would have to let it all out. I will not keep things bottled up any longer. I will address my issues as they arise.

The Last Farewell

Our actions demonstrate the extent of our love for others.

Robbie was making plans to leave for Guyana. I was not sure if it was a permanent or temporary relocation. I hoped he would tell Randy and Sam he was leaving. I did not have the heart to tell them. Robbie had until Friday, August 29, 2008, to leave my home forever.

Finally, the day came. Nothing was packed, nothing to show he was leaving. I heard him get up around 5:30 a.m. I really thought he could not sleep. I got up around 6:00 a.m., made coffee, and had a few words with Randy, who was driving my car to school. I decided I was not going to work. I got dressed to go out to meet a friend for breakfast. I knew it would be difficult to see Robbie's last drive out of my home.

I told Randy to say good-bye to his dad before he left for school, that his dad was leaving today and he wouldn't see him again for a while. Robbie got up as Randy was leaving for school and they hugged. Robbie said nothing to Randy other than, "Just don't mess with the tractor, it cannot be fixed, so don't kill yourself; put a sign on it by the road and say it's for free."

That was all he had to say to his son before he left for Guyana. Randy left. I sat down on the sofa adjacent to Robbie. Sam was still in bed.

"Robbie, I don't have anything more to say other than to take care of yourself," I said.

He started to interject, and I told him to please let me finish.

"I don't know where you got your parenting or partnering skills from, but I am pretty sure it was not your family. Nevertheless, I was willing to overlook a lot and provide you the help you needed to fix yourself. You turned all of it down. I am no longer in a position to deal with this pain anymore. I feel old and beaten down, and each time it's hard for me to pull out. I don't want to feel like this anymore. I am not mad, I am very tired. I want this back-and-forth to end. You knew from the beginning you were not changing and you wasted our time and money. You knew you did not want your family anymore but did not admit it. If you knew you weren't changing, you should have said so and maybe you would have had more money to leave with. That is done now. Leave today, and if you do not leave, I will have you removed and charged with trespassing. I have no choice. I cannot allow this madness to continue. I am very, very tired. You will have your freedom and no one to tell you what to do and when to do it. Go and enjoy your life. I am sorry if I did anything to cause this. I did not mean to. Please forgive me if I did anything. I promise it was not intentional," I said.

I got up and went to the bedroom to put on my makeup after wiping off the tears that were flowing continuously. Robbie came into the room and asked about the bank accounts and that he had a Sears charge coming. He wanted to pay it before he left. I said OK and asked him to give me his card. I called Sears and got the balance due. He sat on the bed while I called. I paid it from his online account. I asked him since he was leaving if he planned to give Randy and Sam any money. He said one thousand dollars each. He asked me to write a check for two thousand dollars and he signed it. I told him thanks and that I would let them know their dad gave them that money.

He asked me to go with him to the bank to help him close some accounts. I said OK and that I would meet him after Sam got on the school bus. I was hoping he would tell Sam he was leaving. I learned from Sam later that he did not tell her.

Next he asked me for a pen to write a withdrawal slip. I gave him the pen. He put on his glasses, and his hands were shaking uncontrollably. I felt true sadness for him. He looked lost. As he was writing I said, "When a person decides to end a marriage, they are ending more than a marriage and some vows; they are ending a lot of other things including the memories and life they shared with another person. You should have considered a lot of things before you decided the marriage was not worth changing for."

He started to cry. He had cried earlier as well when I was talking. I told him he would be crying for a long time, that this was the worst pain he would ever feel, and I was sorry. He did not want the help, and he thought he had no problems, but he did and only he could fix them. I told him the disease of alcoholism is a difficult illness to fight alone.

I left for the bank and he took Sam to the bus stop. I kissed and hugged Sam before I left. Robbie showed up around 9:20 a.m. to meet me. As we were walking in, I told him we were here to transact business and not to go through an emotional crying stage. I told him to hold himself together and get this over with so we could part ways. He looked very, very sad.

We closed his Visa and his checking accounts. He gave me a letter of authorization to close another account in the event he was not able to do so later. We deposited the cash in the children's accounts. I walked out of the bank and leaned against my car; he followed me and stood on the sidewalk. I wanted to cry, but crying did not help, nor did it solve any of my problems. It meant nothing to him or to me anymore. He was sick with the disease, and he could not help himself. I was hoping he would be able to at some point in his life. However, I would choose not to be there to experience it.

"Well, I am going to say good-bye, and this will be the last time you will ever hear me say this. Do the right things by your kids. Make them proud. Now that you are leaving, you might be able to since you won't have the pressures of our relationship to deal with. I am really sorry if I did anything to cause this, but I cannot do any more and I am really tired. As far as you and me, we are over. If in a year or so you happen to be around, we can talk about the kids; but for now, we are done. Good-bye. Here, take this back," I said,

I handed him the wedding ring he had given me at our wedding, the one his parents had made for me, as per our tradition. He left the ring at home and never took it.

I turned around and practically ran to the driver's side door. I got in and drove off. He walked to his car and did the same, and as simple as that, it finally ended. Twenty-one years of hard work for me ended in the blink of an eye. Robbie left our home at 2:15 p.m. on August 29, 2008. This was the last time I saw him for a long time. At 2:45 p.m. he called me several times and could not talk. He was crying. I was crying, not for him but for the loss of a marriage, the loss of a dream. I had no feelings for him, neither love nor hate.

Randy booked a ticket for him to go to New Jersey that night with plans to leave for Guyana soon after that. I was given a ride to the Orlando International Airport to get Robbie's vehicle. Robbie had asked me to pick up his vehicle there. He never told Sam he was leaving. I wanted Sam to tell him good-bye, so I dialed his phone to have Sam talk to him as we drove back home. I could only hear Sam's side of the conversation.

"Hi, Dad, how are you? I wanted to tell you to have a good trip," Sam said.

Thank God it was dark. I was crying silently. I did not want Sam to see me.

"Take care, I love you, Dad," she told him.

I was proud of her. It was dark, and she fell asleep as I was driving. I cried in the dark all the way home. I needed that release at the end of the day. That horrible part of my life was finally over. These tears were ones of relief rather than sadness.

I did not sleep most of the night. I knew I was not going to. I was grieving a loss. It was the death of a dream and a marriage. I'd never wanted this, but I had to stand up for myself and my children and put a stop to what was happening to our lives. I had to stand up to the horrible disease of alcoholism. I was prepared as well as I could be for anything that came my way. I knew it would hurt. I had no idea where my life was going, but I knew where it would never go back. Eventually, I must have fallen asleep.

For me, it took real willpower to change and bend the chronic habits of my mind. Sometimes I still struggle with change. I also believe it takes greater power for an abuser or addict to change in comparison to me. My hope is that my story prompts others to make a change if change is needed, or at least start a change process.

Reflections

Faith is the evidence of things to come.

May God keep Robbie safe and happy. My life is now free of emotional and verbal abuse and free of an alcoholic husband. The horizon of abuse and alcoholism is not visible from where I am standing today. I am on a beautiful side of the horizon. This horizon looks bright and promising. I am walking forward and not looking back. My past will stay in the past, where it belongs. My future is unknown now, but clarity will come when the time is right.

At times, I reflect on the lessons I learned as a young girl combined with adulthood. The lesson of knowing others and their motives. Knowing when to walk away from adversity. Knowing when to question a person's actions when in doubt. Knowing what constitutes abuse. Knowing how alcoholism affected me and my family. Knowing how to be fair and doing the right thing, even if it means being displaced. Knowing when to reach out and ask for help. Finally, knowing when to walk away with grace and dignity, never with resentment.

I consider myself still growing and learning. I do not consider myself an expert on abuse or alcoholism. I consider myself someone who went through a situation with an alcoholic abuser who then applied all I had learned and was taught. I reached out to those more qualified than I for help when I had to. I kept an open mind and worked diligently to keep my morals, ethics, and cultural beliefs intact. I also understand change does not come easily when habits are formed over a lifetime. However, change does come, but that change is an individual one, not predicated by any other person, even those we love. I believe we should change because that change is best for us.

I acknowledge I was an enabler and contributed to Robbie's alcoholism. In the beginning, I did this by denying to myself that he had a drinking problem. Next, I did not seek out help when faced with the symptoms of alcoholism: abuse, lying, threats, or isolation from others. I took on the responsibilities for all expenses, which enabled Robbie to purchase alcohol without worrying about payment of expenses. I also enabled him by traveling often, hence being out of the home. I did not complain when Robbie was not working and was spending almost all his free time out of the home when I was at home. I also was too quick to "rescue" him from reaching his rock bottom. I did this by giving in and feeling remorseful when he would plead and beg for forgiveness. I did not realize then that the disease of alcoholism is sly and cunning. It will say and do anything to get back with its enabler, and when the dust settles, it will rear its ugly head again and again and again. Metaphorically speaking, I watered the tree of alcoholism. I accept full responsibility as an enabler.

There were signs of drunkenness I should have questioned. From the onset of our marriage, Robbie was continuously consuming alcohol and would often display public drunkenness. Starting with our wedding day, Robbie was extremely drunk and argumentative when he learned of the surprise honeymoon arrangements. Soon after that, he was engaged in a furious argument because of drunkenness with one of my uncles, and it resulted in my uncle ending up with a bloody nose. Most evenings after work Robbie would go out drinking and show up drunk at the apartment we shared with my sister and her husband in New York. These were almost daily habits.

When we moved to Florida, I called the Winter Garden Police numerous times to come to the house as a result of Robbie's drunkenness and threats either to himself or to me. An officer once pulled Robbie over in our driveway because the officer observed Robby swerving on the road toward our house. My neighbors would come over and attempt to calm him down, as I was afraid of him when he began arguing. On many occasions, I walked out of the house in order to get out of the environment. Oftentimes he followed me down the road and continued to argue and swear. As the years rolled by, these incidents continued. Visits to parties or social events resulted in Robbie becoming so intoxicated, someone would have to help him into the car. He would later have no recollection of how he got home. Sadly, when close friends and relatives told me that Robbie was drinking a lot and driving drunk, I chose not to believe them.

My synopsis: I believe Robbie was already an alcoholic or an emerging one by the time we were married. If I had not stood up at the onset of physical abuse, I feel he would have continued to be physically abusive as well as verbally abusive. I feel I did everything I could possibly have done to provide the help he needed to stop drinking. In the end, I felt he was not ready to make a change, and I was not prepared to endure the abuse any longer. I believe the disease of alcoholism contributed to most, but not all, of what I experienced. I am still learning each day about alcoholism and its symptoms.

I want to attempt to stop the cycle of abuse and alcoholism from passing to the next generation, my children. I focus on talking about abuse and alcoholism with them. I tell them it is a disease that damages the brain and affects normal functions. I tell them it is a slow, cunning, and progressive disease. The only way to ensure they do not have it is not to consume alcohol on a consistent basis and in high volumes. I am teaching them all I know now and continue to teach them as I am learning. I am not sure if they are listening, but I hope so. Nevertheless, it is my maternal duty to teach them. I hope and pray that eventually they will grow up to lead healthy lives and maintain healthy relationships. I have this wish and hope today. If they do, then I will be confident I was able to break the cycle. If they don't, then I will know I at least tried. In the end, I hope my story will at least inspire one person to make a change in his or her life. It takes one voice, one change, one person to start. This is my wish.

My final reflection: as time went by I had to answer a crucial question to myself. Do I see myself as a victim of abuse? I find it very difficult to admit, but it took me a long time to accept that I am a victim of abuse. I viewed such an admission as a sign of weakness, shame, and failure. Pride, egoism, and denial prevented me from seeing that Robbie was abusing me. I did not want to be portrayed as being a weak person who failed. I am aware of how I felt during the years of my marriage and the pain, suffering, and neglect I endured as a result of the abuse.

I buried the pain and chose not to face it. I was strong on the outside. I managed my professional career with precision, I executed well-thought-out financial decisions, and I played the role of wife and mother the best that I knew how. However, on the inside I was broken, hopeless and in great pain. I felt I had no choice but to accept the situation and I hoped it would vanish one day. I felt if I did not put up a fight my abuser would see me as the good person I am. He would soon discover I meant well and he would stop the abuse. I made excuses for his behavior. I gave in to the abuser and allotted him power over my life. I allowed myself to be abused.

As time went by, I became weaker and I lost my will to fight back. I gradually adapted to the abuse and accepted it as my faith and destiny. I had given up on my abilities to stand up for myself and had very little hope, faith, and trust that the sad situation would change for the better some day. I believe my self-esteem and confidence were lost. The challenge to regain those became my personal mission. Support from those who care for me along with professional help taught me to reacquire my coping and survivor skills. I am the only one that can explain how I felt when being abused. It is very personal and extremely difficult to admit that I allowed someone to abuse me. I unknowingly permitted someone to take away precious years of my youth.

Each of us is different and coping skills are inherently different. I am now aware of this, as I had to face the reality of my situation. I know from experience that physical abuse is not the only form of abuse. I accept that eventually years of abuse eroded my strengths. It slowly and gradually replaced them with weaknesses.

Eventually I was able to attempt to regain my strengths. This happened when I was no longer in denial and when I let go of my pride and ego. That came primarily when I realized that the situation was getting worst and unmanageable. I then reached out and started talking to those more qualified than I. Constant communication with a higher power gave me companionship and brought solace. Those who were knowledgeable about my pain were able to counsel me and guide me into recovery. I was then able to muster the strength and courage I needed to stand up to my abuser. Those and other awakenings encouraged me to make the life-changing decision to protect my children and myself. I did not want my children to feel the pain I felt nor did I want them to emulate the behavior of my abuser. It is my maternal duty to protect my children and to keep them safe from harm. The instinct to protect my children eventually empowered me to make personal changes as well. One of the most profound changes I made was to accept a situation for what it is and not what I wish it or want it to be. Feeling my emotions and reacting to them in such a manner as to bring about positive outcomes is by far the biggest change I have gone through. In am confident I can change, but that change has to be right for me.

Today, looking back at everything that happened and getting back into finding myself, I am sure I regained my love for and trust in others. This I am sure of, just as I am sure the sun will rise each morning. I am sure my life will be lived the way a life should be lived, not dictated by abuse and alcoholism. I am a patient person. I also have time on my side. Yes, time is what I have. This is all I need for today. Just for today, I have peace. Just for today, I have happiness. Just for today, I am smiling.

I summarize the journey I took as walking a path of goodness and love, and in the end, it seems other forces made their entries into my life as if to help and urge me along the path of peace and happiness. I am happy that I was able to share my journey with you.

Epilogue

It has been a few years since my marriage ended. I've spent most of the time completing my book and working toward publishing while bringing awareness to others about abuse as it relates to alcoholism. I have also been busy raising my two children, and reconnecting with family and friends while establishing new friendships.

Randy graduated from high school in June 2010. He is currently enrolled in a local college with hopes pursuing a college degree. Sam started high school in 2010 and is enjoying her time. They are both very outgoing and a lot more talkative than they used to be. They no longer walk around the house as if they were walking on eggshells. I feel they are much more relaxed and happy.

At the time of this publication I am still the Senior Finance and Accounting Manager for Starwood Vacation Ownership, Inc., a division of Starwood Hotels and Resorts Worldwide. I have no current plans to make a career change.

In addition to learning more about the disease of alcoholism, I also spent a considerable amount of time getting to know me, as an individual, again. I learned a lot about myself and will share those lessons with you in the future. I will remain connected with my readers and supporters in the years to come.

I continue to educate myself on what constitutes emotional and verbal abuse and how it impacted me. Other than the first onset of physical abuse early in the marriage there was no other physical violence. I was not black and blue. I have no broken bones. During the many years of my marriage I was made to feel that I was not a good wife, that my life and friends were worthless and that I did not come from a good family.

I learned through my personal struggles that this type of abuse is serious, but often overlooked due to the fact that there are no physical or external signs as in the physical abuse. The results of verbal and emotional abuse, however, are just as real as the effects of physical abuse. I believe the scars are made at a different level of our being. The years of this type of abuse caused me to start believing that I was not good, my family was not good; my friends only wanted to 'use' me, and my life had no value. It eroded my sense of self worth and self esteem. It was an awful feeling, a feeling I wish upon no one.

I learned that a person who degrades or embarrasses another is being emotionally abusive. This can be done through excessive criticism, name calling and talking down to a person. If a person tries to keep another away from family and friends, then I think it may be the onset of abuse. In my case, I believe my abuser's objectives were to isolate me, and keep me away from those who could have helped me. This isolation enabled my abuser to control me as well as keeping me from those who truly care for my well-being. If I was around someone who cared, I probably would have been able to seek help and leave earlier.

I learned that being around him induced a lot of fear in me. I was afraid of upsetting him. I think this was a clear sign that the relationship was not healthy. At first I did not see this as abuse and brushed it off as 'bad temper' or 'his personality.' I made countless excuses for his unacceptable behaviors and lied to those close to me in order to protect his privacy. I felt it was my duty to save him or help him change. Many times, as helpless as I was, I felt that I could not live without him. In my case the effects of emotional and verbal abuse were devastating and I felt they were even more long lasting than I originally believed when I exited the relationship. I still feel sad for me when I reflect on my feelings during the abusive years. At times I do cry for what I endured.

There is a broad shady line, I believe, between a healthy argument and abuse. In any relationship, there will be disputes and arguments. Those can be healthy if expressed in the right manner. A couple who can recognize each other's different needs, views or wishes will certainly argue or discuss, but things are likely to be worked out in the end. Arguments don't have to be shouting matches. They can simply be a means used to convince someone of something which is important and which we feel strongly about. Healthy arguments should *never* lead to any physical, verbal or emotional bashing.

There are several tools available to abuse victims today, including support groups and counseling as well as utilizing the massive amount of information available on the internet. I used those learning tools and many

Epilogue

more, including talking to others with similar experiences. I bonded with those who truly care and accepted their support while gaining the strength to move forward. These people helped me to slowly move out of the world of abuse and into a more beautiful and peaceful world; a world where I can offer some help to others who may be in similar situations.

Helpful Information

United States

The National Domestic Violence Hotline
1-800-799-7233
1-800-787-3224(TTY)
http://www.thehotline.org/get-help/help-in-your-area/#F

Organizations in Guyana I have partnered with thus far

IMRARC
011-592-257-0912
imrarccanegrove@yahoo.com

Kids First Fund
011-592-226-5926
011-592-226-6231
011-592-226-6214
011-592-623-8505
kidsfirstfund@hotmail.com
www.kidsfirstfundguyana.org

Facebook Sites
Breakout by Sukree Boodram: A true story
Stop the violence against women in Guyana

Other Websites
www.sukreeboodram.com
blog.sukreeboodram.com

Other contact
sukree@sukreeboodram.com
sukreeboodram@yahoo.com
stoptheviolenceGY@gmail.com

Notes

Notes

www.ingramcontent.com/pod-product-compliance
Lightning Source LLC
Chambersburg PA
CBHW032041090426
42744CB00004B/84